Get Smart: Building Bulletproof Web3 Smart Contract Applications with Solidity

Pete Cox

Published by Northwood Lore Books, 2024.

GET SMART: BUILDING BULLETPROOF WEB3 SMART CONTRACT APPLICATIONS WITH SOLIDITY

First edition. November 18, 2024.

ISBN: 979-8230687337

Written by Pete Cox.

Table of Contents

1. Introduction to Secure Smart Contract Development

Smart contract security is not just a technical requirement but a fundamental necessity in the blockchain ecosystem. As we embark on this comprehensive journey through secure smart contract development, it's crucial to understand that the immutable and financial nature of blockchain applications makes security paramount. Unlike traditional software where bugs can be patched post-deployment, smart contract vulnerabilities can lead to irreversible losses of funds and trust. This chapter sets the foundation for understanding the critical importance of security in smart contract development and introduces the key principles that will guide us throughout this book.

The blockchain landscape has witnessed numerous high-profile security incidents that have resulted in hundreds of millions of dollars in losses. From the infamous DAO hack that led to the Ethereum hard fork to more recent DeFi protocol exploits, these incidents serve as stark reminders of the consequences of inadequate security measures. Smart contracts, once deployed, become permanent fixtures on the blockchain, making it crucial to get security right from the start. This immutability, while being one of blockchain's greatest strengths, also means that developers must adopt a security-first mindset from the earliest stages of development.

Security in smart contract development encompasses multiple layers and considerations. At the most fundamental level, developers must understand the unique characteristics of blockchain platforms and how they differ from traditional computing environments. The Ethereum Virtual Machine (EVM) operates in a deterministic, resource-constrained environment where every operation has a cost in terms of gas. This economic model introduces new security considerations that developers must account for, such as potential denial of service attacks through gas manipulation or front-running attacks due to the public nature of pending transactions.

One of the primary challenges in secure smart contract development is the need to anticipate and protect against various attack vectors. Smart contracts operate in an adversarial environment where any vulnerability can and will be exploited. Attackers are highly motivated, often with significant financial resources at their disposal, and have the advantage of being able to study deployed contract code extensively. This reality necessitates a comprehensive security approach that combines proper coding practices, thorough testing, and formal verification methods.

The principles of secure smart contract development begin with code simplicity and clarity. Complex systems are inherently more difficult to secure and more prone to bugs. Developers should strive to write clear, straightforward code that can be easily audited and understood by others. This includes following established patterns and best practices, using well-tested libraries, and avoiding unnecessary complexity. The principle of least privilege should be applied rigorously, ensuring that contract functions and users have only the minimum necessary permissions to perform their intended actions.

Another crucial aspect of smart contract security is the proper implementation of access controls and permission systems. Smart contracts often need to manage valuable assets and perform privileged operations, making it essential to have robust mechanisms for controlling who can execute specific functions and under what conditions. This includes implementing proper role-based access control systems, multi-signature requirements for critical operations, and emergency stop mechanisms that can halt contract operations in case of detected vulnerabilities.

Testing plays a vital role in secure smart contract development. Unlike traditional software testing, smart contract testing must be exhaustive and consider various attack scenarios. This includes unit testing individual components, integration testing of contract interactions, and specific security-focused testing to identify potential vulnerabilities. Automated testing tools, formal verification methods, and manual code reviews all play important roles in ensuring contract security. Additionally, developers must consider the economic implications of their contracts, testing not just for functional correctness but also for economic security under various market conditions.

Gas optimization, while often considered a performance concern, is also a security consideration. Poorly optimized contracts can be vulnerable to denial of service attacks or may become unusable during periods of high network congestion. Developers must carefully balance security measures with gas efficiency, ensuring that security features don't make the contract prohibitively expensive to use while maintaining necessary protections.

The development environment and tooling choices also impact security. Using mature, well-tested development frameworks and tools can help avoid common pitfalls and provide additional security guarantees. This includes choosing appropriate compilers, development environments, and testing frameworks. Version control practices, deployment procedures, and continuous integration pipelines should all be designed with security in mind.

Documentation plays a crucial role in secure smart contract development. Clear, comprehensive documentation helps prevent misunderstandings that could lead to security vulnerabilities and assists in the audit process. This includes both technical documentation of the code itself and higher-level documentation explaining the contract's purpose, assumptions, and security model.

As we progress through this book, we will explore each of these aspects in detail, providing practical examples and battle-tested patterns for implementing secure smart contracts. We will examine common vulnerabilities and their prevention, study successful security patterns, and learn how to prepare contracts for professional security audits. The goal is to equip developers with the knowledge and tools necessary to create secure, reliable smart contracts that can withstand the test of time and potential attacks.

The field of smart contract security is constantly evolving, with new vulnerabilities being discovered and new security patterns being developed. Successful smart contract developers must commit to continuous learning and staying informed about the latest security developments in the ecosystem. This includes following security researchers, participating in the developer community, and regularly reviewing post-mortems of security incidents to learn from others' experiences.

Throughout this book, we will maintain a practical focus, providing concrete examples and real-world scenarios that illustrate security concepts. Each chapter builds upon the previous ones, gradually developing a comprehensive understanding of smart contract security. By the end of this journey, readers will have the knowledge and tools necessary to develop secure smart contracts and the ability to evaluate and improve the security of existing contracts.

Remember that security is not a destination but a continuous process. Even the most carefully designed smart contracts can have vulnerabilities, and new attack vectors are constantly being discovered. The key is to approach smart contract development with a security-first mindset, implement proper security measures, and maintain vigilance throughout the contract's lifecycle. With the foundation laid in this introduction, we are ready to delve deeper into the specific aspects of secure smart contract development in the following chapters.

2. Understanding the Ethereum Virtual Machine (EVM)

The Ethereum Virtual Machine (EVM) serves as the computational engine that powers smart contract execution on the Ethereum blockchain. Understanding its architecture, capabilities, and limitations is crucial for developing secure smart contracts. The EVM is a quasi Turing-complete state machine that executes contract bytecode in a deterministic, isolated environment, ensuring that identical inputs always produce the same outputs across all network nodes.

At its core, the EVM operates on a stack-based architecture, managing program execution through a simple last-in-first-out (LIFO) data structure. This stack can hold up to 1024 elements, each 256 bits wide, reflecting Ethereum's fundamental data size. Understanding this limitation is crucial for security, as attempting to exceed the stack depth can cause contract execution to fail, potentially leading to unexpected behavior if not properly handled.

The EVM's memory model consists of three distinct areas: stack, memory, and storage. The stack is used for immediate computations and is highly gas efficient but limited in size. Memory is a linear, byte-addressable space that exists only during contract execution and is cleared between calls. Storage is permanent and persists on the blockchain, making it the most expensive resource in terms of gas costs. Each storage slot is 256 bits, and while this provides ample space for most data types, improper storage patterns can lead to significant gas inefficiencies and potential security vulnerabilities.

Gas mechanics play a fundamental role in EVM security. Every operation executed by the EVM consumes gas, with costs varying based on computational complexity and resource usage. This economic model serves multiple purposes: it prevents infinite loops, ensures fair compensation for network nodes, and creates an upper bound on computation. However, it also introduces security considerations. Contracts must be designed to handle out-of-gas scenarios gracefully, as running out of gas during execution will revert all state changes but consume the gas provided.

The EVM's execution context provides important security guarantees. Each contract execution runs in an isolated environment, with strict controls on how contracts can interact with each other. This isolation helps prevent many types of attacks common in traditional computing environments, but developers must still be careful about cross-contract interactions. The EVM provides special opcodes for external calls (CALL, DELEGATECALL, and STATICCALL), each with different security implications that must be thoroughly understood.

Bytecode execution in the EVM follows a deterministic path, with each opcode performing a specific function. The EVM includes approximately 140 opcodes, ranging from simple arithmetic operations to more complex operations like cryptographic functions. Understanding how these opcodes work and their gas costs is essential for writing secure and efficient contracts. For example, the SSTORE opcode, used for writing to storage, is one of the most expensive operations, while simple stack operations like PUSH and POP are relatively cheap.

The EVM's handling of data types and type safety deserves special attention. While Solidity provides high-level abstractions, the EVM itself operates only on 256-bit words. This can lead to subtle bugs when dealing with smaller data types or when performing type conversions. Understanding how the EVM handles different data types and their representations is crucial for preventing overflow, underflow, and type confusion vulnerabilities.

Contract creation and deployment in the EVM follows a specific process. When a contract is deployed, its constructor code is executed once, and the resulting runtime bytecode is stored on the blockchain. This immutable nature of deployed code means that any bugs or vulnerabilities in the runtime code become permanent features of the contract. Understanding this deployment process and the distinction between creation-time and runtime code is essential for implementing secure initialization patterns and upgrade mechanisms.

The EVM's error handling mechanism is relatively simple: any error condition causes the entire transaction to revert, rolling back all state changes but consuming the gas used up to the point of failure. This all-or-nothing approach provides strong atomicity guarantees but requires careful consideration in contract design, particularly when implementing complex multi-step operations or handling external calls.

Memory management in the EVM requires careful attention. While memory is cheaper than storage, it expands quadratically in terms of gas costs. This can lead to denial-of-service vulnerabilities if contracts allow unbounded memory growth. Additionally, memory layout and alignment can impact gas costs and should be optimized while maintaining security.

The EVM's event logging system provides a way to emit information that is stored in the blockchain's transaction logs but not in contract storage. While events don't affect contract execution, they are crucial for off-chain applications and contract monitoring. Proper use of events can enhance contract security by providing audit trails and enabling external monitoring systems to detect suspicious activities.

Understanding the EVM's precompiled contracts is also important for security. These are special contracts that provide optimized implementations of commonly used cryptographic functions. While they offer better performance than implementing the same functions in Solidity, their use cases and limitations must be well understood to avoid security pitfalls.

The deterministic nature of the EVM has important implications for random number generation and timing-dependent operations. True randomness cannot be achieved within the EVM alone, and block timestamps can be manipulated within certain bounds by miners. Understanding these limitations is crucial for designing secure contracts that require randomness or time-based logic.

The EVM's account model, which distinguishes between externally owned accounts (EOAs) and contract accounts, influences how contracts can interact with the broader Ethereum ecosystem. Understanding the differences between these account types and their capabilities is essential for implementing secure authentication and authorization mechanisms.

State management in the EVM requires careful consideration. Contract state must be managed carefully to prevent unauthorized access or modification. The EVM's storage model, where each storage slot is accessible by any function unless explicitly restricted by high-level language constructs, means that proper access controls must be implemented at the contract level.

Looking ahead, the EVM continues to evolve with new improvements and features being proposed and implemented. Staying informed about these changes is crucial for security, as new EVM features may introduce both opportunities for improved security and new potential vulnerabilities to consider.

In conclusion, a deep understanding of the EVM is fundamental to developing secure smart contracts. Its unique characteristics and constraints shape how we must approach security in smart contract development, influencing everything from basic arithmetic operations to complex cross-contract interactions. As we progress through this book, we'll build upon this foundation to explore specific security patterns and best practices that leverage our understanding of the EVM's capabilities and limitations.

3. Solidity Language Fundamentals

Building upon our understanding of the EVM, let's explore the fundamental elements of the Solidity programming language that form the basis for secure smart contract development. Solidity is a statically typed, contract-oriented language specifically designed for writing smart contracts on the Ethereum platform and other EVM-compatible blockchains.

Data types in Solidity form the foundation of contract state and logic. The language provides several primitive types, including uint and int in various bit sizes (uint8 through uint256), bool for boolean values, address for Ethereum addresses, and bytes for raw byte data. Understanding the nuances of these types is crucial for security. For instance, using uint256 instead of smaller integer types can prevent overflow issues in many cases, though it comes with slightly higher gas costs.

Variables in Solidity can have different visibility levels and storage locations. State variables are permanently stored in contract storage and can be public, private, or internal. Memory variables exist only during function execution, while storage variables persist between function calls. The correct choice of storage location is crucial for both security and gas efficiency. Improperly managing storage variables can lead to significant vulnerabilities, particularly when dealing with complex data structures.

Functions are the primary means of interacting with smart contracts. Solidity supports several function types, including view functions that read but don't modify state, pure functions that neither read nor modify state, and regular functions that can modify state. Function visibility modifiers (public, external, internal, and private) control how functions can be accessed, forming a crucial part of the contract's security model. External functions can only be called from outside the contract, while public functions can be called both internally and externally.

Modifiers are a powerful feature in Solidity that allow for code reuse and enhanced security checks. They can be used to implement access control, validate inputs, or ensure certain conditions are met before function execution. However, modifiers must be used carefully, as they can make code flow harder to follow and potentially introduce reentrancy vulnerabilities if not properly implemented.

Events in Solidity provide a way to log important contract state changes and actions. They are essential for contract monitoring and off-chain applications. Properly designed events can serve as an audit trail and help detect potential security incidents. Events are also gas efficient compared to storing the same information in contract storage, making them an attractive option for logging non-critical data.

Error handling in Solidity has evolved significantly. The language provides require(), assert(), and revert() statements for different error scenarios. require() is used for input validation and checking conditions that should be met for normal operation, assert() is used for internal consistency checks and invariants, and revert() allows for custom error handling. Proper error handling is crucial for contract security, as it helps prevent invalid state transitions and provides clear feedback about failure conditions.

Inheritance is a key feature in Solidity that enables code reuse and the implementation of upgrade patterns. Multiple inheritance is supported, with contracts able to inherit from multiple parent contracts. The order of inheritance matters due to Solidity's C3 linearization rules. Understanding these rules is essential when implementing complex inheritance hierarchies, particularly in upgradeable contract systems.

Interfaces and abstract contracts provide ways to define contract interactions and implement design patterns. Interfaces contain function signatures without implementations, while abstract contracts can include both implemented and unimplemented functions. These features are crucial for building modular, secure contract systems and implementing proxy patterns.

Solidity's type system includes several advanced features that require careful consideration. Fixed-point numbers are not fully supported, leading developers to implement their own fixed-point arithmetic libraries. String handling is relatively basic, and string operations can be gas intensive. Arrays and mappings are the primary data structures available, each with their own security considerations regarding iteration and access patterns.

Memory management in Solidity requires careful attention. Dynamic arrays and strings in memory can lead to gas issues if not properly managed. The language's reference types (arrays, structs, and mappings) have different behavior depending on whether they're stored in memory or storage, which can lead to subtle bugs if not properly understood.

Function calls in Solidity can be low-level (address.call()) or high-level (contract interface calls). Low-level calls provide more flexibility but require careful handling of return values and error conditions. High-level calls provide better type safety but may hide complexity that needs to be considered for security.

The language includes special functions like receive() and fallback() that handle incoming Ether transfers and unknown function calls. These functions must be implemented carefully to prevent security issues, particularly in contracts that need to handle Ether transfers or interact with other contracts.

Assembly blocks in Solidity provide direct access to EVM operations. While they can be useful for gas optimization and implementing certain low-level operations, they bypass Solidity's safety checks and should be used with extreme caution. Incorrect use of assembly can introduce serious vulnerabilities.

Constants and immutable variables provide gas-efficient ways to store values that don't change. Constants must be set at compile time, while immutable variables can be set during contract construction. Using these features appropriately can improve contract security by preventing accidental state changes.

User-defined value types, introduced in recent Solidity versions, allow for creating more type-safe contracts by wrapping primitive types with specific semantic meaning. This feature can help prevent errors caused by mixing up similar but semantically different values.

The language continues to evolve with new features and improvements in each release. Staying current with Solidity developments is crucial for security, as newer versions often include important security improvements and new features that can help write more secure contracts.

Understanding these language fundamentals is essential for implementing secure smart contracts. Each feature must be used with careful consideration of its security implications, keeping in mind the unique constraints and requirements of blockchain-based applications. As we progress through more advanced topics, this foundation will be crucial for understanding and implementing secure smart contract patterns and practices.

4. Development Environment Setup

Setting up a robust development environment is crucial for secure smart contract development. A well configured environment helps catch potential vulnerabilities early in the development process and provides the tools necessary for thorough testing and debugging.

The foundation of any Solidity development environment starts with Node.js and npm (Node Package Manager). These tools are essential for managing project dependencies and running development scripts. While not directly related to blockchain development, they form the backbone of most modern development toolchains. Install the latest LTS (Long Term Support) version of Node.js, as it provides the best balance of features and stability.

Truffle Suite has long been the go to development framework for Ethereum smart contracts. It provides a comprehensive set of tools for compilation, deployment, testing, and debugging. The Truffle framework includes a built in testing framework, a network management system, and a development console for interacting with deployed contracts. Installing Truffle globally via npm makes it available throughout your system: npm install -g truffle. However, consider using a local installation per project to ensure version consistency across team members.

Hardhat has emerged as a powerful alternative to Truffle, gaining significant popularity in recent years. It offers superior debugging capabilities, faster compilation times, and better support for modern JavaScript features. Hardhat's configuration system is more flexible than Truffle's, allowing for complex deployment scenarios and custom task definitions. The Hardhat Network, a local Ethereum network node designed for development, provides detailed error messages and stack traces that are invaluable for debugging.

Code editors play a crucial role in catching potential issues before they make it into production. Visual Studio Code has become the de facto standard for Solidity development, thanks to its extensive ecosystem of extensions. The Solidity extension by Juan Blanco provides syntax highlighting, code completion, and inline compilation errors. Additionally, the Solidity Visual Developer extension offers visual security warnings and best practice suggestions directly in the editor.

Local blockchain networks are essential for development and testing. Ganache, part of the Truffle Suite, provides a personal blockchain for Ethereum development. It allows developers to deploy contracts, develop applications, and run tests in a safe, deterministic environment. Ganache is available both as a command line tool and a graphical application, making it accessible for developers with different preferences.

Version control is non negotiable for secure development. Git should be used to track changes and collaborate with team members. Configure your .gitignore file properly to exclude sensitive information like private keys and environment files. Consider using git hooks to run automated tests and linting before commits are allowed.

Environment management is critical for security. Never store sensitive information like private keys or API endpoints directly in your code. Use environment variables and configuration files to manage different settings for development, testing, and production environments. The dotenv package is commonly used to manage environment variables in Node.js projects.

Testing tools are essential components of the development environment. In addition to the testing frameworks provided by Truffle and Hardhat, consider installing specific security testing tools. Slither, a static analysis framework, can identify many common vulnerabilities. MythX provides comprehensive security analysis through its API, though it requires a subscription for full access.

Contract verification tools should be part of your environment setup. Etherscan's verification service allows users to verify that deployed bytecode matches your source code. Tools like hardhat-etherscan automate this process, making it easier to maintain transparency and trust in your deployed contracts.

Gas optimization tools help ensure your contracts are cost effective to deploy and use. The hardhat-gas-reporter plugin provides detailed gas usage reports for your contract functions. solidity-coverage helps ensure your tests cover all possible execution paths, which is crucial for security.

Documentation tools help maintain clear and accurate documentation, which is essential for security audits and maintenance. Solidity's natspec comments are the standard for contract documentation. Tools like soldoc can generate documentation from these comments automatically.

Linting tools help maintain code quality and catch potential issues early. Solhint and Ethlint (formerly Solium) are popular choices for Solidity linting. Configure these tools with appropriate rule sets that align with your team's coding standards and security requirements.

Debugging tools are crucial for understanding contract behavior. Remix IDE, while primarily web based, provides excellent debugging capabilities and can be integrated into your local development environment. The hardhat-debugger plugin offers similar functionality within the Hardhat environment.

Monitoring tools help track contract behavior in production. Set up logging systems that can track important contract events and alert you to potential issues. Tools like Tenderly provide real time monitoring and alerting for smart contracts.

Package management requires careful consideration. While npm is used for JavaScript dependencies, managing Solidity package dependencies requires additional tools. OpenZeppelin's contracts are essential for secure development and can be installed via npm, but verify all imported code carefully.

Continuous Integration (CI) tools help maintain code quality across a team. Configure GitHub Actions or similar CI systems to automatically run tests, security checks, and linting on every pull request. This helps catch issues before they make it into production code.

Development networks should be properly configured for different stages of development. Local networks like Hardhat Network for development, test networks like Sepolia or Goerli for integration testing, and proper production networks for deployment should all be properly configured in your development environment.

Wallet integration is necessary for testing and deployment. MetaMask is essential for browser based testing, while tools like hardhat-ledger enable hardware wallet integration for secure deployment to production networks.

Security tools should be integrated into your development workflow. Regular vulnerability scanning, static analysis, and fuzzing tests should be easy to run from your development environment. Configure these tools to run automatically when possible.

Your development environment should also include tools for gas estimation and optimization. Understanding the gas costs of your contracts is crucial for both security and usability. Tools should be configured to provide accurate gas estimates for your target networks.

Remember that a development environment is not static it should evolve with your project's needs and as new tools become available. Regularly review and update your tools and configurations to ensure you're using the most secure and efficient options available.

5. Smart Contract Architecture Principles

Smart contract architecture principles form the foundation of secure and maintainable decentralized applications. A well-architected smart contract system follows established patterns while remaining flexible enough to accommodate future changes and upgrades. This chapter explores the core principles that should guide your contract architecture decisions.

Modularity stands as one of the most critical principles in smart contract architecture. Breaking down complex systems into smaller, focused contracts not only makes the code more manageable but also reduces the attack surface of each component. Each contract should have a single, well-defined responsibility. For example, rather than creating one massive contract that handles token logic, access control, and business operations, separate these concerns into distinct contracts that interact through clearly defined interfaces.

The separation of concerns principle closely relates to modularity but focuses on keeping different aspects of the system independent. Storage contracts should be separated from logic contracts, authentication should be handled independently from business logic, and administrative functions should be isolated from user-facing operations. This separation makes the system easier to upgrade, test, and secure. It also allows for better access control as different components can have different permission levels.

Inheritance hierarchies should be carefully planned and limited in depth. While Solidity supports multiple inheritance, deep inheritance chains can lead to complexity and potential security vulnerabilities. The diamond pattern or proxy patterns often provide better alternatives for complex systems than deep inheritance hierarchies. When using inheritance, follow the Liskov Substitution Principle ensure that derived contracts can truly substitute for their base contracts without breaking the system's functionality.

State management requires careful consideration in smart contract architecture. Every storage slot used in a contract costs gas, and state variables persist on the blockchain permanently. Design your contract's state structure to minimize storage operations and optimize gas usage. Consider using mapping structures instead of arrays where possible, and be mindful of packing variables to save storage slots. However, never sacrifice clarity and security for minor gas optimizations.

Events play a crucial role in smart contract architecture. They provide an efficient way to communicate state changes to off-chain systems and serve as an audit trail for contract operations. Design your event structure carefully, including all relevant information while being mindful of gas costs. Events should be emitted for all significant state changes and important operations, allowing external systems to track contract activity effectively.

Access control architecture requires careful planning from the start. Implement a robust permission system that can accommodate future needs while remaining secure and gas efficient. Consider using role-based access control (RBAC) patterns rather than simple owner patterns, as they provide more flexibility and granular control. Always follow the principle of least privilege, granting only the minimum necessary permissions to each role or address.

Interface definitions serve as contracts between different system components. Well-defined interfaces make it easier to upgrade individual components without affecting the entire system. Use interface inheritance to maintain consistency across different implementations, and document interface requirements thoroughly. Consider using the ERC standards where applicable, as they provide well-tested interface definitions for common functionality.

Error handling architecture should be consistent throughout your system. Define custom errors for specific failure conditions rather than using generic revert messages. This not only saves gas but also provides better feedback to users and calling contracts. Design your error handling to fail early and explicitly, checking preconditions at the start of functions rather than allowing operations to proceed with invalid states.

Upgradeability patterns should be considered from the beginning of architecture design, even if immediate upgradeability is not required. The ability to fix bugs or add features after deployment can be crucial for long-lived contracts. However, upgradeability adds complexity and potential security risks, so carefully weigh the tradeoffs. Consider using transparent proxy patterns or the diamond pattern for upgradeability, depending on your specific requirements.

Gas optimization should be built into the architecture rather than added as an afterthought. Design function signatures to minimize input data size, optimize storage layouts to reduce gas costs, and consider batch operations for frequent transactions. However, maintain a balance between gas optimization and code readability. Complex optimizations that make code difficult to understand often lead to security vulnerabilities.

External contract interactions should be carefully architected to maintain security. Follow the checks-effects-interactions pattern to prevent reentrancy attacks. Design your contract interfaces to be resistant to malicious external contracts, and always assume that external calls might fail. Consider implementing circuit breakers or rate limiting mechanisms for external interactions.

Factory patterns can provide powerful deployment and management capabilities. Design factory contracts to create and track instances of your main contracts, allowing for easier management and upgradeability. Factory patterns can also help with permission management and contract discovery, but ensure they don't introduce unnecessary complexity or security risks.

Data structures should be chosen based on their specific use cases and security implications. Arrays versus mappings, simple versus complex structures, memory versus storage usage all these decisions impact both security and gas costs. Design data structures to minimize state changes and storage operations while maintaining data integrity and access efficiency.

Cross contract communication patterns should be carefully designed to maintain system security and efficiency. Consider using a facade pattern to provide a simple interface to complex systems, and implement proper access controls for cross contract calls. Design your communication patterns to be resistant to malicious contracts and handle failure cases gracefully.

Testing considerations should influence your architecture decisions. Design your contracts to be easily testable, with clear interfaces and state isolation. Consider implementing view functions that expose internal state for testing purposes, but ensure these cannot be misused in production. Structure your contracts to allow for comprehensive unit testing of individual components and integration testing of the complete system.

Documentation forms an essential part of contract architecture. Design your contracts with clear documentation in mind, using meaningful names and consistent patterns. Implement thorough natspec comments explaining not just what functions do, but why certain architectural decisions were made. Good documentation helps with maintenance, auditing, and future upgrades.

6. Common Smart Contract Vulnerabilities Overview

Smart contract vulnerabilities represent one of the most critical challenges in blockchain development, with millions of dollars lost due to exploits and bugs. Understanding common vulnerabilities is essential for any developer working with smart contracts, as it forms the foundation for writing secure code and implementing effective preventive measures.

Reentrancy vulnerabilities remain among the most notorious security issues in smart contracts. These occur when a contract calls an external contract before resolving its own state changes, allowing the external contract to recursively call back into the vulnerable contract. The infamous DAO hack of 2016, which resulted in the loss of approximately 3.6 million ETH, exploited this vulnerability. Developers must implement proper guards and follow the checks effects interactions pattern to prevent reentrancy attacks.

Integer overflow and underflow vulnerabilities arise from the limitations of fixed size variables in Solidity. Prior to Solidity 0.8.0, arithmetic operations could silently wrap around when exceeding their maximum or minimum values, leading to unexpected behavior. While newer versions of Solidity include built in checks, developers must remain vigilant when working with arithmetic operations, especially when interacting with older contracts or implementing custom mathematical functions.

Access control vulnerabilities often stem from inadequate permission systems or incorrectly implemented access restrictions. Unprotected initialization functions, missing ownership checks, and improper role management can all lead to unauthorized access to critical contract functions. These vulnerabilities can be particularly devastating as they often give attackers complete control over contract functionality and assets.

Front running vulnerabilities occur in blockchain systems due to the public nature of transaction pools. Malicious actors can observe pending transactions and submit their own transactions with higher gas prices to execute before the original transactions. This vulnerability is particularly relevant in decentralized exchanges and other systems where transaction ordering matters.

Logic errors represent a broad category of vulnerabilities resulting from flawed business logic implementation. These can include incorrect state transitions, improper validation of inputs, or mishandled edge cases. While not technically exploits, logic errors can lead to significant losses and often require careful auditing and testing to identify.

Storage manipulation vulnerabilities arise when contracts fail to properly protect their state variables. Uninitialized storage variables, improper storage slots usage, and inadequate access controls on state modifying functions can all lead to unauthorized state modifications. These vulnerabilities often result from a poor understanding of Solidity's storage mechanics.

Timestamp manipulation vulnerabilities occur when contracts rely on block timestamps for critical operations. Miners can manipulate timestamps within certain bounds, making them unreliable for precise timing requirements. Contracts should avoid depending on exact timestamp values and instead use block numbers or other more reliable mechanisms for timing sensitive operations.

Gas related vulnerabilities can manifest in several ways. Loops with unbounded iterations can cause transactions to fail due to exceeding block gas limits. Insufficient gas stipends for external calls can prevent contracts from executing as intended. Developers must carefully consider gas consumption patterns and implement appropriate limits and checks.

External call vulnerabilities arise from interactions with other contracts. Failed calls, malicious contracts, and unexpected behavior can all lead to vulnerabilities. Contracts should implement proper error handling for external calls, validate responses, and protect against potential malicious behavior from called contracts.

Denial of service vulnerabilities can occur when contracts allow users to block the execution of critical functions. This might happen through gas exhaustion attacks, deliberately failed transactions, or manipulation of contract state to prevent further operations. Proper gas limits, circuit breakers, and careful state management are essential to prevent these attacks.

Privacy vulnerabilities stem from the public nature of blockchain data. All contract data and interactions are visible on the blockchain, potentially exposing sensitive information. While some privacy can be achieved through commitment schemes and other cryptographic techniques, developers must carefully consider what information they store on chain.

Upgradeability vulnerabilities often occur in contracts implementing proxy patterns or other upgradeability mechanisms. Storage collisions, improper initialization, and flawed access controls in upgrade mechanisms can lead to serious vulnerabilities. Careful implementation and thorough testing of upgradeability patterns is essential.

Cross contract vulnerability occurs when contracts interact with multiple other contracts in complex ways. Race conditions, unexpected state changes, and circular dependencies can all lead to vulnerabilities. Proper architecture and careful consideration of inter contract interactions are necessary to prevent these issues.

Oracle manipulation vulnerabilities arise when contracts rely on external data sources. Malicious or compromised oracles can feed incorrect data to contracts, leading to unexpected behavior.

Implementing proper oracle security measures and using decentralized oracle networks can help mitigate these risks.

Token related vulnerabilities include issues specific to ERC20, ERC721, and other token standards. These can include approval racing, transfer validation bugs, and other standard specific issues. Developers must thoroughly understand the token standards they implement and follow established best practices.

Flash loan vulnerabilities have become increasingly common in DeFi applications. These attacks leverage large amounts of borrowed assets within a single transaction to manipulate prices or exploit other vulnerabilities. Proper price oracle implementation and transaction ordering protection can help prevent these attacks.

Compiler level vulnerabilities can arise from using outdated or buggy compiler versions, or from misunderstanding compiler optimizations and features. Staying current with compiler updates and understanding compiler behavior is essential for preventing these issues.

The evolving nature of smart contract vulnerabilities requires constant vigilance and continuous learning. New attack vectors are discovered regularly, and existing protections may become insufficient as the ecosystem evolves. Developers must stay informed about new vulnerabilities and regularly update their security practices.

Testing for vulnerabilities requires a comprehensive approach combining unit tests, integration tests, and specialized security tools. Automated vulnerability scanners, formal verification tools, and manual code review all play important roles in identifying potential security issues before they can be exploited.

7. Reentrancy Attacks and Prevention

Reentrancy attacks represent one of the most devastating vulnerabilities in smart contract development, having led to numerous high-profile exploits and substantial financial losses in the blockchain ecosystem. This chapter delves deep into understanding reentrancy vulnerabilities, their various manifestations, and proven prevention techniques that developers can implement to protect their smart contracts.

At its core, a reentrancy attack occurs when a malicious contract exploits the ability to recursively call back into a vulnerable contract before the first invocation completes its execution. This vulnerability typically manifests when a contract sends Ether or tokens to an external address before updating its internal state. The receiving contract can then call back into the vulnerable contract, finding it in an inconsistent state, and potentially drain funds through repeated recursive calls.

The classic example of a reentrancy vulnerability involves a simple withdrawal function in a contract that manages user balances. Consider a contract that first sends Ether to a user and then updates their balance. If the recipient is a malicious contract, its fallback function can call back into the withdrawal function before the balance is updated, allowing multiple withdrawals of the same funds. The infamous DAO hack of 2016, which resulted in the loss of approximately 3.6 million ETH, exploited precisely this type of vulnerability.

Reentrancy attacks can manifest in several forms. Single-function reentrancy, as described above, occurs when an attacker repeatedly calls the same vulnerable function. Cross-function reentrancy happens when an attacker reenters the contract through a different function that shares state with the original vulnerable function. Read-only reentrancy involves exploiting inconsistent state during view functions, which can be particularly dangerous in DeFi applications where these functions often determine crucial parameters like exchange rates or collateral requirements.

The Checks Effects Interactions (CEI) pattern represents the primary defense against reentrancy attacks. This pattern dictates that contract functions should first perform all necessary checks (preconditions, validations), then make any required state changes (effects), and finally interact with external contracts or addresses (interactions). By following this pattern, even if an external call leads to reentrant behavior, the contract's state will already have been updated, preventing exploitation.

Implementation of the CEI pattern requires careful attention to function structure. All state changes should occur before any external calls. For example, in a withdrawal function, the user's balance should be reduced before sending Ether. This ensures that even if the recipient contract attempts to reenter, the reduced balance will prevent additional withdrawals. Additionally, developers should consider implementing reentrancy guards, which use modifiers to prevent any reentrant calls to protected functions.

The OpenZeppelin ReentrancyGuard contract provides a battle-tested implementation of reentrancy protection. This contract uses a simple but effective mutex pattern, setting a boolean flag before function execution and clearing it afterward. Any attempt at reentrant calls will fail as the flag check will prevent multiple simultaneous executions of protected functions.

Cross-contract reentrancy requires special attention, particularly in complex DeFi protocols where multiple contracts interact with each other. Developers must carefully analyze all possible interaction paths between contracts and ensure that state changes across the entire system maintain consistency. This often involves implementing protocol-wide reentrancy guards and carefully managing the order of operations across contract boundaries.

Flash loan attacks have introduced new variations of reentrancy vulnerabilities. These attacks combine the power of flash loans with reentrancy to manipulate market prices or exploit other vulnerabilities within a single transaction. Preventing these attacks requires not only traditional reentrancy protection but also careful consideration of price oracle implementations and economic incentives within the system.

Static analysis tools can help identify potential reentrancy vulnerabilities during development. Tools like Slither and Mythril can automatically scan contract code for common reentrancy patterns. However, these tools should complement, not replace, careful code review and testing, as complex reentrancy vulnerabilities might not be detected through automated analysis alone.

Testing for reentrancy vulnerabilities requires specific attention in the contract's test suite. Developers should write tests that attempt to exploit potential reentrancy vulnerabilities, including creating mock attacking contracts that try to reenter protected functions. These tests should verify that the contract's state remains consistent even under attempted reentrancy attacks.

Future developments in Ethereum and Solidity may introduce new mechanisms for preventing reentrancy attacks. For example, proposals for atomic transactions and new EVM features could provide additional tools for developers to protect against these vulnerabilities. However, understanding and properly implementing current best practices remains crucial for secure smart contract development.

When auditing contracts for reentrancy vulnerabilities, developers should pay particular attention to functions that send Ether or tokens, interact with external contracts, or modify state after external calls. Each such function should be analyzed for potential reentrancy vectors, considering both direct and cross-function reentrancy possibilities.

Documentation plays a crucial role in preventing reentrancy vulnerabilities. Functions that interact with external contracts should clearly document their assumptions about reentrancy protection and any requirements for secure usage. This documentation helps future maintainers understand the security implications of code modifications and helps auditors focus their attention on critical areas.

As smart contract complexity increases, new forms of reentrancy vulnerabilities may emerge. Developers must stay informed about new attack vectors and regularly review their reentrancy protection mechanisms. Regular security audits, continuous monitoring, and prompt response to discovered vulnerabilities remain essential practices for maintaining secure smart contracts in an evolving ecosystem.

8. Integer Overflow and Underflow Protection

Integer overflow and underflow vulnerabilities have historically been among the most common and dangerous issues in smart contract development. While Solidity version 0.8.0 introduced built-in overflow checking for arithmetic operations, understanding these vulnerabilities remains crucial for maintaining secure contracts, especially when working with older codebases or when explicit unchecked operations are required for gas optimization.

An integer overflow occurs when an arithmetic operation attempts to create a numeric value that exceeds the maximum value that can be stored in the allocated memory. Conversely, an underflow happens when an operation results in a value below the minimum representable value. In Solidity, different integer types have different ranges, with uint256 being the most commonly used, supporting values from 0 to 2^256 - 1.

Before Solidity 0.8.0, a simple addition operation could silently overflow, wrapping around to zero or a small number, potentially with catastrophic consequences. Consider a token contract where a user's balance overflows due to a large transfer. The overflow could result in the user having fewer tokens than before, breaking the fundamental accounting of the contract. Similarly, underflow vulnerabilities could allow users to spend more tokens than they possess by exploiting arithmetic operations that wrap around to large numbers when going below zero.

The introduction of automatic overflow checking in Solidity 0.8.0 was a significant improvement for contract security. When an overflow or underflow occurs, the contract execution reverts, preventing silent failures. However, developers must remain vigilant for several reasons. First, many deployed contracts still use older Solidity versions without these protections. Second, developers might deliberately use unchecked blocks for gas optimization, requiring careful manual validation. Third, interaction with external contracts might involve calculations that bypass these checks.

For contracts using Solidity versions prior to 0.8.0, the SafeMath library from OpenZeppelin became the de facto standard for safe arithmetic operations. SafeMath provides functions that check for overflow and underflow conditions before performing calculations, reverting the transaction if a violation occurs. While SafeMath adds some gas overhead, its security benefits far outweigh the costs in most scenarios.

Implementing proper integer overflow protection requires a systematic approach to arithmetic operations throughout the contract. Developers should identify all locations where numeric calculations occur and ensure appropriate safeguards are in place. This includes not only direct mathematical operations but also operations that might indirectly affect numeric values, such as array length calculations or gas calculations.

A common pattern for protecting against overflow and underflow involves implementing input validation before performing calculations. For example, when implementing a transfer function in a token contract, the code should verify that the sender's balance is sufficient and that the transfer amount plus the recipient's current balance won't overflow. These checks should be performed as early as possible in the function to fail fast and save gas.

Gas considerations play a significant role in overflow protection strategies. While automatic checks provide security, they come with increased gas costs. In performance-critical sections of code where the developer can mathematically prove that overflow is impossible, using unchecked blocks can optimize gas usage. However, such optimizations should be thoroughly documented and carefully reviewed to ensure they don't introduce vulnerabilities.

Testing for overflow and underflow vulnerabilities requires comprehensive test cases that explore boundary conditions. Tests should verify behavior at the maximum and minimum values for each numeric type used in the contract. Additionally, fuzz testing can help identify edge cases by automatically generating random inputs that might trigger overflow conditions.

When dealing with external contracts or user inputs, developers should be particularly cautious about arithmetic operations. Malicious actors might attempt to manipulate input values to trigger overflows in seemingly safe calculations. Implementing strict input validation and using safe arithmetic operations becomes crucial in these scenarios.

Complex mathematical operations require special attention. Operations involving multiplication are particularly prone to overflow, as numbers can grow exponentially. When performing calculations with multiple steps, developers should carefully consider the order of operations to minimize the risk of intermediate results overflowing. In some cases, using alternative calculation methods or breaking down operations into smaller steps can help avoid overflow conditions.

Decimal handling in Solidity presents additional challenges related to overflow protection. Since Solidity doesn't support floating-point numbers, developers typically use fixed-point arithmetic with integer scaling factors. These calculations require careful attention to prevent overflow both in the intermediate steps and final results. Libraries like PRBMath provide safe fixed-point arithmetic operations that handle these cases correctly.

Contract upgrades and modifications must maintain consistent overflow protection throughout the system. When adding new functionality or modifying existing code, developers should ensure that all mathematical operations remain protected against overflow and underflow. This includes reviewing any assumptions about value ranges and updating validation checks accordingly.

Documentation plays a vital role in maintaining secure arithmetic operations. Code comments should clearly indicate any assumptions about value ranges and explain why specific arithmetic operations are safe. When using unchecked blocks for optimization, the documentation should provide mathematical proofs or explanations of why overflow is impossible in those cases.

Auditing for integer overflow vulnerabilities involves both automated and manual review processes. Static analysis tools can identify potential overflow conditions, but human review remains essential for understanding the business logic and validating that all mathematical operations are properly protected. Auditors should pay particular attention to complex calculations, especially those involving user inputs or external contract interactions.

As smart contract ecosystems evolve, new patterns and tools for handling integer arithmetic continue to emerge. Developers should stay informed about best practices and new security considerations related to overflow protection. Regular code reviews and updates to security measures help ensure that contracts remain protected against these fundamental vulnerabilities.

9. Access Control Patterns

Access control patterns form the backbone of smart contract security, establishing who can perform specific actions within a contract and under what conditions. These patterns are essential for maintaining the integrity and security of decentralized applications by preventing unauthorized access to critical functions and protecting sensitive data.

The most fundamental access control pattern is the Ownable pattern, which designates a single address as the contract owner with special privileges. This pattern is implemented through a state variable storing the owner's address and modifiers that restrict function access to the owner. While simple, the Ownable pattern provides a foundation for more complex access control mechanisms and is particularly useful for administrative functions like pausing contracts or updating configuration parameters.

However, relying solely on a single owner creates centralization risks and potential single points of failure. To address these concerns, developers often implement more sophisticated access control patterns that distribute privileges across multiple addresses or roles. The multi signature pattern, for example, requires multiple authorized parties to approve sensitive operations before they can be executed, significantly reducing the risk of unauthorized actions.

Role based access control (RBAC) extends basic ownership concepts by defining multiple roles with different permission levels. Each role represents a set of allowed actions, and addresses can be assigned to one or more roles. This granular approach allows for fine tuned permission management and better reflects real world organizational structures. Common roles might include administrators, operators, maintainers, and users, each with specific capabilities and restrictions.

Access control patterns should implement secure role management functions. This includes carefully controlled methods for adding and removing role members, transferring role assignments, and renouncing roles. These functions must include appropriate checks and balances to prevent privilege escalation or unauthorized role modifications. For example, the ability to assign new administrators should typically require approval from multiple existing administrators.

Time based access control adds another dimension to permission management. Contracts can implement temporary permissions that expire after a certain period or restrict certain actions to specific time windows. This pattern is particularly useful for scheduled maintenance operations or gradual privilege transitions. Developers must ensure that time based restrictions cannot be circumvented through manipulation of block timestamps or other timing attacks.

Implementing hierarchical access control allows for the creation of permission trees where higher level roles inherit the capabilities of lower level roles while maintaining additional privileges. This pattern mirrors traditional organizational structures and simplifies permission management in complex systems. Care must be taken to prevent circular dependencies or unintended privilege escalation through role inheritance.

Emergency access patterns provide mechanisms for handling critical situations while maintaining security. These might include emergency admin roles that can only be activated under specific conditions or through multi signature approval. Such patterns should be carefully designed to prevent abuse while ensuring they remain effective when needed during genuine emergencies.

Delegation patterns allow role holders to temporarily grant their permissions to other addresses without permanently transferring their role. This flexibility is valuable for operational efficiency but requires careful implementation to prevent permission leakage or unauthorized delegation chains. Time limits and revocation mechanisms are essential components of secure delegation systems.

Access control patterns must also consider gas efficiency. Checking role assignments and permissions adds overhead to function calls, so optimizations are important for frequently called functions. Techniques like bitmap based role storage and efficient permission checking algorithms can significantly reduce gas costs while maintaining security.

Smart contracts often need to interact with other contracts, requiring cross contract access control patterns. These patterns must ensure that permissions are properly validated across contract boundaries and that malicious contracts cannot exploit trust relationships. Implementing secure callback patterns and maintaining careful control over external contract interactions is crucial.

Upgradeability considerations are particularly important for access control patterns. When contracts are upgraded, access control states must be preserved correctly, and new security measures must be backward compatible with existing role assignments. Upgrade mechanisms themselves should be protected by robust access controls to prevent unauthorized modifications.

Event logging plays a crucial role in access control systems. All significant permission changes should emit events that can be monitored off chain. This creates an audit trail of role assignments and permission modifications, facilitating oversight and allowing for quick detection of unauthorized changes. Events should include sufficient detail to reconstruct the full history of access control changes.

Testing access control patterns requires comprehensive coverage of both positive and negative cases. Tests should verify that authorized users can perform allowed actions while unauthorized attempts are properly rejected. Edge cases, such as role revocation during pending operations or complex interaction sequences, deserve particular attention.

Documentation of access control patterns should clearly specify the permission model, including all roles, their capabilities, and the procedures for role management. This documentation serves as both a security reference and a guide for contract maintainers. Special attention should be paid to documenting emergency procedures and the rationale behind permission structures.

Modern smart contract development frameworks provide reusable implementations of common access control patterns. OpenZeppelin's AccessControl contract, for example, offers a standardized, audited implementation of role based access control. While these libraries provide a solid foundation, developers must understand their underlying mechanisms and carefully consider whether additional customization is needed for specific use cases.

The evolution of decentralized autonomous organizations (DAOs) has introduced new requirements for access control patterns. These systems often need to implement complex voting mechanisms and permission structures that reflect democratic or stake weighted governance models. Access control patterns for DAOs must balance security with flexibility and community participation.

Monitoring and maintenance of access control systems requires ongoing attention. Regular audits of role assignments, automated monitoring of permission changes, and periodic reviews of access patterns help ensure continued security as systems evolve. Maintenance procedures should themselves be subject to appropriate access controls while remaining practical for legitimate administrative needs.

10. Role-Based Permissions Implementation

Role based permissions implementation builds upon basic access control patterns by providing a structured framework for managing complex permission hierarchies in smart contracts. This chapter explores the practical implementation details and best practices for creating robust role based permission systems.

At the core of role based permissions is the concept of distinct roles that encapsulate specific sets of permissions. Each role represents a collection of allowed actions or access rights within the contract system. Implementation typically begins with defining an enumeration or mapping of roles, each identified by a unique identifier. These identifiers can be implemented as bytes32 values, which provide a good balance between storage efficiency and readability.

The foundational data structure for role based permissions consists of a nested mapping that associates addresses with roles and roles with permissions. This can be implemented using a double mapping structure where the first level maps roles to addresses, and the second level tracks whether those addresses have the specified role. Additional mappings can associate roles with specific permissions or capabilities, creating a flexible and extensible permission system.

A crucial aspect of implementing role based permissions is the initialization of the system. The contract deployer or initial administrator must be assigned appropriate roles during contract creation. This is typically handled in the constructor, where the deploying address is granted administrative privileges. Care must be taken to ensure that this initial setup cannot be manipulated and that the contract cannot enter a state where no address has administrative capabilities.

Role management functions form the backbone of the implementation. These include functions for granting roles, revoking roles, and checking role assignments. Each of these functions must include appropriate access controls to ensure that only authorized addresses can modify role assignments. A common pattern is to require that role management functions can only be called by addresses with administrative privileges or through a governance mechanism.

The implementation of role checks within contract functions typically uses modifiers to enforce permission requirements. These modifiers verify that the calling address has the required role before allowing function execution. Multiple modifiers can be combined to create complex permission requirements, such as requiring multiple roles or implementing role hierarchies where higher level roles inherit permissions from lower level roles.

Error handling in role based permission systems requires careful consideration. When unauthorized access attempts occur, the contract should revert with clear, specific error messages that help users and developers understand why the operation failed. Custom error types can be defined to provide detailed information about permission failures while maintaining gas efficiency.

Role hierarchies add another layer of complexity to the implementation. These hierarchies allow certain roles to inherit permissions from other roles, creating a tree like structure of capabilities. Implementation requires careful tracking of role relationships and efficient methods for checking whether a role inherits specific permissions. Circular dependencies in role hierarchies must be prevented through proper validation during role relationship setup.

Temporary role assignments introduce time based elements to the permission system. This requires additional storage for tracking assignment durations and expiration timestamps. The implementation must include mechanisms for automatically revoking expired roles and preventing actions when roles have expired. Time based permissions should use block timestamps consistently and account for potential manipulation of block timestamps by miners.

Role transfer functionality allows for the controlled handover of responsibilities between addresses. This requires implementing secure transfer mechanisms that prevent roles from being lost or stolen. A common pattern is the two step transfer process where the current role holder initiates a transfer and the new address must accept it explicitly. This prevents accidental transfers to invalid or inaccessible addresses.

Batch operations for role management can improve efficiency when dealing with multiple role assignments or revocations. However, these batch operations must maintain the same security guarantees as individual operations. Implementation should include proper validation of all operations in the batch and atomic execution to prevent partial state changes.

Event emission is essential for tracking role changes and maintaining an audit trail. Events should be emitted for all significant role operations, including grants, revocations, and transfers. These events should include sufficient information to reconstruct the complete history of role assignments and changes, facilitating off chain monitoring and analysis.

Gas optimization in role based permission systems requires careful balance between functionality and efficiency. Bitmap based role storage can reduce gas costs for multiple role assignments to the same address. Caching frequently checked role assignments in memory during complex operations can also improve efficiency. However, these optimizations must not compromise the security of the permission system.

Integration with external systems requires careful consideration of cross contract permission checking. When contracts interact, role based permissions must be properly validated across contract boundaries. This might involve implementing interfaces for role checking or maintaining synchronized role states across multiple contracts.

Testing role based permission implementations requires comprehensive coverage of various scenarios. Tests should verify proper role assignment, permission inheritance, role revocation, and interaction between different roles. Edge cases such as role expiration during ongoing operations or complex permission combinations need particular attention.

Documentation of role based permission systems should clearly specify the available roles, their relationships, and associated permissions. This includes detailed descriptions of role management functions, permission requirements for various operations, and procedures for role transfers and revocations. Clear documentation helps prevent misunderstandings that could lead to security issues.

Upgradeability considerations for role based permissions require careful handling of role state during upgrades. The implementation should include mechanisms for preserving role assignments when contract logic is upgraded. This might involve separate storage contracts for role data or careful state migration procedures.

Monitoring and maintenance of role based permission systems requires ongoing attention. The implementation should include tools and interfaces for administrators to review current role assignments, check permission relationships, and audit recent changes. Regular verification of role states helps ensure the system remains secure and properly configured.

The implementation of role based permissions must also consider potential attack vectors such as front running of role assignments or permission changes. Proper transaction ordering and access controls around role management functions help prevent manipulation of the permission system. Additional safeguards might include time locks on sensitive role changes or multi signature requirements for critical operations.

Integration with governance systems adds another dimension to role based permission implementation. This might involve connecting role management to voting systems or other decentralized decision making mechanisms. The implementation must ensure that governance driven role changes maintain the same security properties as direct administrative actions.

11. Secure Function Execution Patterns

Secure function execution patterns form a critical foundation for building robust and reliable smart contracts. These patterns ensure that contract functions behave predictably, handle errors gracefully, and maintain security invariants throughout their execution. Understanding and implementing these patterns is essential for developing trustworthy decentralized applications.

The Checks Effects Interactions pattern stands as one of the most fundamental secure execution patterns. This pattern dictates that function execution should follow a specific order: first perform all necessary checks and validations, then modify contract state, and finally interact with external contracts or addresses. Following this pattern helps prevent reentrancy attacks and ensures that contract state remains consistent even if external calls fail.

Input validation represents the first line of defense in secure function execution. Every parameter passed to a function should be thoroughly validated before processing. This includes checking for zero addresses, verifying numerical ranges, validating array lengths, and ensuring string inputs meet required formats. Input validation should be comprehensive but gas efficient, striking a balance between security and cost.

State validation forms another crucial aspect of secure function execution. Before processing a function, the contract must verify that its current state allows for the intended operation. This includes checking contract balances, verifying timing conditions, and ensuring that state variables meet required conditions. State validation helps prevent operations from executing in invalid contexts or unexpected states.

Function modifiers play a vital role in implementing secure execution patterns. They provide a clean, reusable way to implement common checks and validations. However, modifiers must be used carefully to maintain code clarity and prevent unexpected interactions between multiple modifiers. The order of modifier execution should be carefully considered, as it can affect the overall security of the function.

Error handling patterns determine how functions respond to invalid conditions or failed operations. Rather than using require statements with string messages, modern Solidity contracts should utilize custom errors to provide detailed failure information while optimizing gas usage. Error conditions should be specific and informative, helping users and developers understand exactly why an operation failed.

The Check Effects Interactions pattern particularly shines in functions that handle asset transfers or interact with external contracts. These functions should always update internal state before initiating external transfers or calls. This ensures that the contract's state remains consistent even if external operations fail or behave maliciously. Additionally, any necessary events should be emitted after state changes but before external interactions.

Reentrancy guards represent another essential execution pattern, particularly for functions that interact with external contracts. While the Checks Effects Interactions pattern provides some protection against reentrancy, explicit guards offer an additional layer of security. These guards typically use a boolean flag or counter to track function execution status and prevent reentrant calls.

Function visibility plays a crucial role in secure execution patterns. Internal functions should be used for logic that doesn't need external access, while public and external functions should be carefully designed to maintain security boundaries. Private functions can encapsulate sensitive operations that should never be accessible outside the contract.

Return value handling requires careful attention, particularly when dealing with external calls. Low level calls should always have their return values checked to ensure successful execution. Functions should handle both successful and failed states appropriately, maintaining contract integrity regardless of external operation outcomes.

Gas considerations influence secure function execution patterns. Functions should be designed to fail early if conditions aren't met, preventing unnecessary gas consumption. Complex operations should be broken down into smaller, more manageable steps when possible, allowing users to better predict and manage gas costs.

State machine patterns often complement secure function execution by ensuring that functions can only execute in appropriate contract states. These patterns use explicit state tracking and transitions to prevent invalid operation sequences. Functions should verify current state requirements and properly update state variables when executing state transitions.

Atomic execution patterns ensure that functions either complete successfully or revert entirely, leaving no partial state changes. This atomicity is particularly important for functions that perform multiple related operations. All state changes within a function should be designed to maintain consistent contract state, even if the function reverts.

Event emission patterns provide transparency and auditability for function execution. Events should be emitted at appropriate points during function execution to record significant state changes or important operations. The timing of event emission should be consistent with the Checks Effects Interactions pattern to maintain proper execution order.

Secure delegation patterns become relevant when functions need to execute logic in other contracts. These patterns should include proper access controls, careful handling of return values, and protection against malicious contract behavior. Delegation should be implemented in a way that maintains the security properties of the calling contract.

Function composition patterns help manage complexity in contracts with sophisticated logic. Breaking down complex operations into smaller, well defined functions improves code readability and maintainability. However, care must be taken to ensure that the interaction between these functions maintains security invariants and doesn't introduce vulnerabilities.

Circuit breaker patterns provide emergency control over function execution. These patterns allow for graceful handling of critical situations by including mechanisms to pause or restrict function execution when necessary. Implementation should include proper access controls for circuit breaker activation and clear conditions for resuming normal operation.

Initialization patterns ensure that contract functions begin execution in a valid state. This includes proper constructor initialization, validation of initial state variables, and protection against uninitialized storage variables. Functions should verify that necessary initialization has occurred before allowing execution of contract logic.

The implementation of secure function execution patterns requires careful testing and validation. Each pattern should be thoroughly tested under various conditions, including edge cases and potential attack scenarios. Documentation should clearly explain the security properties provided by each pattern and any assumptions about their usage.

12. Safe Mathematical Operations

Mathematical operations in smart contracts require special attention to security due to the potential for overflow, underflow, and precision loss. These vulnerabilities can lead to serious financial losses and contract malfunctions if not properly handled. This chapter explores comprehensive approaches to implementing safe mathematical operations in Solidity smart contracts.

The fundamental challenge with mathematical operations in smart contracts stems from the limitations of fixed size integer types. Solidity integers, whether signed or unsigned, have specific maximum and minimum values. When operations exceed these boundaries, traditional programming languages might throw exceptions, but the EVM historically would simply wrap around, potentially leading to catastrophic results in financial calculations.

SafeMath libraries emerged as the primary solution for secure mathematical operations in Solidity versions prior to 0.8.0. These libraries provided wrapper functions for basic arithmetic operations that included overflow and underflow checks. While SafeMath is less critical in modern Solidity versions that include built in overflow checking, understanding its principles remains valuable for working with legacy code and implementing custom mathematical operations.

Modern Solidity (version 0.8.0 and later) includes built in overflow checking for all arithmetic operations. This means that operations that would result in overflow or underflow automatically revert the transaction. While this provides a basic level of security, developers still need to carefully consider how to handle these cases in their application logic. Simply relying on transaction reverts may not provide the best user experience.

Division operations require particular attention in smart contracts. Integer division in Solidity truncates towards zero, which can lead to precision loss. When dealing with financial calculations, this precision loss can accumulate and cause significant discrepancies. A common pattern is to use a fixed point decimal system, typically with 18 decimal places (similar to Ether's wei denomination), to maintain precision in calculations.

Multiplication operations present their own challenges, particularly when dealing with large numbers or percentages. A common pattern is to perform multiplication before division to maintain precision. However, this approach must be balanced against the risk of intermediate overflow. Careful ordering of operations and appropriate scaling factors become crucial in these scenarios.

Percentage calculations require special consideration in smart contracts. A naive implementation might lose significant precision or produce incorrect results. The standard pattern involves multiplying the base number by the percentage first, then dividing by 100 (or 10000 for basis points). However, this must be implemented carefully to avoid overflow in the intermediate multiplication step.

Fixed point arithmetic becomes necessary when dealing with non integer values in smart contracts. Since Solidity doesn't natively support floating point numbers, developers must implement fixed point arithmetic using integer mathematics. This typically involves scaling numbers by a fixed factor (like 10^18) and implementing carefully designed functions for multiplication, division, and other operations that maintain this scale factor appropriately.

Rounding in mathematical operations needs explicit handling in smart contracts. Different financial applications may require different rounding behaviors (round up, round down, or round to nearest). These rounding decisions can have significant implications for token economics and should be carefully considered and documented.

Gas optimization becomes particularly relevant when implementing safe mathematical operations. While safety is paramount, the implementation must also consider the gas costs of different approaches. For instance, using multiplication followed by division might be more gas efficient than multiple separate division operations, but the implementation must still guard against overflow in the intermediate steps.

Working with extremely large numbers often requires special handling. This might involve breaking calculations into smaller steps, using appropriate scaling factors, or implementing custom data structures for handling large numbers. The choice of approach depends on the specific requirements of the application and the constraints of the platform.

Negative numbers require careful consideration in smart contracts. While signed integers are available in Solidity, many financial calculations work better with unsigned integers and explicit handling of negative cases. This often involves designing data structures and algorithms that handle negative values through application logic rather than relying on signed arithmetic.

Mathematical libraries play a crucial role in implementing safe operations. Beyond basic arithmetic, these libraries often provide functions for more complex operations like exponentiation, square roots, logarithms, and trigonometric functions. When implementing or using such libraries, careful validation of their security properties and edge cases is essential.

Testing mathematical operations requires comprehensive coverage of edge cases and boundary conditions. This includes testing with maximum and minimum values, testing around overflow and underflow boundaries, and verifying precision in fixed point calculations. Property based testing can be particularly valuable for identifying edge cases in mathematical operations.

Error handling for mathematical operations should be explicit and informative. Custom error types can provide detailed information about why a calculation failed, helping users and developers understand and address issues. The error handling strategy should consider both technical correctness and user experience.

Documentation of mathematical operations should be particularly thorough, including clear explanations of any assumptions, limitations, or special cases. This includes documenting the precision guarantees of fixed point operations, the handling of edge cases, and any rounding behaviors. Such documentation is crucial for both security audits and long term maintenance.

The implementation of secure mathematical operations often requires balancing multiple concerns: security, precision, gas efficiency, and user experience. A well designed implementation will consider all these factors while providing clear documentation and comprehensive testing. As smart contracts continue to handle increasingly complex financial operations, the importance of secure mathematical implementations only grows.

13. Gas Optimization Fundamentals

Gas optimization is a critical aspect of smart contract development that directly impacts the cost and efficiency of decentralized applications. Understanding and implementing gas optimization fundamentals ensures that your smart contracts remain economically viable while maintaining their intended functionality and security.

Gas in Ethereum represents the computational cost of executing operations on the blockchain. Every operation in the EVM consumes a specific amount of gas, from basic arithmetic to storage operations. Users must pay for this gas in ETH, making optimization not just a technical consideration but an economic imperative.

Storage operations are among the most gas intensive operations in smart contracts. Writing to storage (SSTORE) costs significantly more gas than reading from storage (SLOAD). A fundamental optimization principle is to minimize storage operations whenever possible. This can be achieved by carefully designing data structures and utilizing memory for intermediate calculations.

The use of proper data types plays a crucial role in gas optimization. Smaller uint types like uint8 or uint16 might seem more gas efficient, but this is often a misconception. The EVM operates on 256 bit words, and using smaller types can actually increase gas consumption due to the additional operations required for packing and unpacking values. Unless there's a specific reason to use smaller types, uint256 is generally the most gas efficient choice.

Loop optimization is another fundamental consideration. Loops can quickly consume large amounts of gas, especially when they involve storage operations or complex calculations. Breaking loops early when possible, caching array lengths outside the loop, and using memory arrays instead of storage arrays within loops can significantly reduce gas consumption. However, developers must be careful not to introduce vulnerabilities when optimizing loops.

Function modifiers can impact gas consumption in unexpected ways. The view and pure modifiers signal that a function doesn't modify state, allowing these calls to be executed without gas costs when called externally. However, when these functions are called internally from other functions, they still consume gas. Understanding these nuances helps in designing more gas efficient contract architectures.

String operations in Solidity are particularly gas intensive. Minimizing string manipulation, using bytes32 instead of string when possible, and careful management of dynamic string arrays can lead to significant gas savings. When string operations are necessary, implementing them efficiently requires understanding the underlying byte manipulation operations.

Event logging presents opportunities for gas optimization. While events are crucial for off chain monitoring and user interfaces, they consume gas. Carefully selecting which data to include in events and using indexed parameters efficiently can reduce gas costs while maintaining necessary functionality.

Variable packing is an advanced optimization technique that takes advantage of how the EVM handles storage slots. Multiple variables can be packed into a single 256 bit storage slot if their combined size is less than or equal to 256 bits. However, proper alignment is crucial for this optimization to be effective. Careful ordering of state variables can lead to significant gas savings through efficient packing.

Function visibility modifiers affect both security and gas consumption. External functions can be more gas efficient than public functions when called with calldata arguments. Understanding when to use external versus public, and private versus internal, can lead to meaningful gas savings while maintaining proper access control.

Batch operations can significantly reduce gas costs when multiple similar operations need to be performed. Instead of executing multiple separate transactions, implementing batch processing functions allows multiple operations to share fixed gas costs like transaction overhead and storage slot access.

Memory management is crucial for gas optimization. While memory is much cheaper than storage, it isn't free. Efficient memory usage involves minimizing allocations, reusing memory space when possible, and being mindful of memory expansion costs. Understanding how the EVM manages memory helps in writing more gas efficient code.

Constant and immutable variables provide gas savings by avoiding storage operations. Values that don't change should be declared as constant or immutable whenever possible. The difference between these declarations lies in when the value is set: constants at compile time, immutable during construction.

Assembly can be used for extreme gas optimization cases. While inline assembly should be used sparingly due to its complexity and potential for introducing vulnerabilities, it can provide significant gas savings for specific operations. Common use cases include efficient memory operations and bit manipulation.

Function parameters and return values affect gas consumption. Using calldata for external function parameters, minimizing the number of parameters and return values, and efficiently structuring complex parameter types can all contribute to gas savings. The trade off between gas efficiency and code readability must be carefully considered.

Error handling mechanisms have different gas implications. Custom errors, introduced in Solidity 0.8.4, are more gas efficient than revert strings. However, the choice between different error handling approaches should consider both gas efficiency and the need for clear error messages.

Testing gas optimization requires specific tools and approaches. Gas reporters in testing frameworks can help track the gas consumption of different functions and identify optimization opportunities. Regular gas profiling during development helps maintain efficiency as contracts evolve.

Documentation of gas optimization strategies is essential for maintaining and upgrading contracts. Clear comments explaining optimization choices help future developers understand the reasoning behind specific implementations and avoid accidentally introducing inefficiencies during modifications.

The balance between optimization and readability requires careful consideration. While aggressive gas optimization might reduce costs, it can make code harder to maintain and audit. The appropriate level of optimization depends on the specific requirements of each project and the expected usage patterns of the contract.

Gas optimization is an ongoing process that requires regular monitoring and adjustment. As network conditions and gas prices change, different optimization strategies may become more or less important. Maintaining flexibility in contract design allows for adaptation to changing conditions while preserving core functionality.

14. Advanced Gas Optimization Techniques

Advanced gas optimization techniques build upon fundamental principles to achieve even greater efficiency in smart contract execution. These sophisticated approaches require a deep understanding of the EVM and careful consideration of trade-offs between optimization and code maintainability.

Contract deployment optimization is a crucial but often overlooked aspect of gas efficiency. The deployment bytecode size directly affects deployment costs, and various techniques can reduce this overhead. Removing unnecessary functions, optimizing constructor logic, and carefully managing initialization parameters can significantly reduce deployment costs. Libraries can be particularly useful for reducing deployment costs when similar code is used across multiple contracts, as the library code only needs to be deployed once.

Bit manipulation provides powerful optimization opportunities when dealing with boolean flags or small numeric values. Instead of using multiple boolean storage variables, packing them into a single uint256 using bitwise operations can dramatically reduce storage costs. This technique requires careful implementation to maintain readability and avoid errors, but the gas savings can be substantial for contracts that manage multiple flags or states.

Advanced storage patterns can yield significant gas savings. The storage pointer technique allows for efficient access to deeply nested mappings by calculating storage slots directly rather than through multiple accesses. Similarly, implementing custom packed storage structures can optimize gas usage beyond simple variable packing by carefully arranging data to minimize storage operations.

Dynamic array optimization requires sophisticated approaches beyond basic loop optimization. Implementing pagination for large arrays, using merkle trees for verification of large datasets, and implementing efficient search algorithms can dramatically reduce gas costs for operations on large collections. When dealing with dynamic arrays, consider implementing lazy deletion patterns where items are marked as deleted rather than actually removed, saving gas by avoiding array reorganization.

Advanced memory management techniques can provide substantial gas savings in complex contracts. Implementing memory pools for frequently allocated structures, reusing memory space for intermediate calculations, and carefully managing memory layout can reduce gas costs associated with memory operations. Understanding the EVM's memory expansion costs helps in optimizing memory usage patterns.

Assembly level optimizations can provide significant savings when implemented correctly. Custom memory management through assembly, efficient storage slot access patterns, and optimized mathematical operations can reduce gas costs beyond what's possible with high level Solidity. However, these optimizations require extensive testing and should be clearly documented to maintain code safety and maintainability.

Proxy contract optimization presents unique challenges and opportunities. Implementing efficient delegate call patterns, optimizing storage layouts for upgradeable contracts, and carefully managing initialization logic can reduce gas costs in proxy architectures. Understanding storage slot collision risks and implementing proper storage patterns for upgradeable contracts is crucial for maintaining both efficiency and security.

Event optimization goes beyond basic event emission. Implementing efficient event filtering patterns, optimizing indexed parameter usage, and carefully managing event data structure can reduce gas costs while maintaining necessary functionality. Consider implementing batched event emission for high frequency operations to reduce overall gas costs.

Function selector optimization can provide meaningful gas savings in contracts with many functions. Organizing function selectors efficiently, implementing optimized dispatcher patterns, and carefully managing function visibility can reduce execution costs. Understanding how the EVM handles function selection helps in implementing these optimizations effectively.

State access optimization patterns can significantly reduce gas costs in complex contracts. Implementing caching mechanisms for frequently accessed state, optimizing state access patterns in loops, and carefully managing state updates can provide substantial gas savings. Consider implementing batch state update patterns for operations that modify multiple state variables.

Mathematical optimization techniques beyond basic safe math operations can provide significant savings. Implementing efficient algorithms for complex calculations, optimizing division operations, and carefully managing precision in fixed point arithmetic can reduce gas costs while maintaining accuracy. Understanding the gas costs of different mathematical operations helps in choosing optimal implementation patterns.

Calldata optimization techniques can reduce gas costs for contracts that handle complex input data. Implementing efficient parameter packing, optimizing array handling in calldata, and carefully managing dynamic types can provide meaningful savings. Understanding how the EVM handles calldata helps in implementing these optimizations effectively.

Cross contract call optimization requires careful consideration of both gas costs and security implications. Implementing efficient batch call patterns, optimizing parameter passing between contracts, and carefully managing return data can reduce gas costs in complex contract systems. Consider implementing caching mechanisms for frequently accessed external contract data.

Gas token integration provides opportunities for advanced gas cost management. Implementing efficient gas token minting and burning patterns, optimizing storage refund mechanisms, and carefully managing gas token balance can provide economic benefits in certain scenarios. Understanding network gas price dynamics helps in implementing effective gas token strategies.

Compiler optimization techniques can provide additional gas savings. Understanding and properly configuring compiler optimization settings, implementing efficient inheritance patterns, and carefully managing contract size can reduce deployment and execution costs. Regular testing with different compiler versions and optimization settings helps identify optimal configurations.

These advanced optimization techniques must be implemented thoughtfully, with careful consideration of their impact on contract security and maintainability. Proper testing, documentation, and code review processes are essential when implementing advanced gas optimizations. Regular monitoring and adjustment of optimization strategies ensures continued efficiency as network conditions and contract usage patterns evolve.

The implementation of advanced gas optimization techniques should be guided by specific contract requirements and usage patterns. Not all optimization techniques are appropriate for every contract, and the benefits of complex optimizations must be weighed against their implementation and maintenance costs. Maintaining a balance between optimization and code clarity ensures long term contract sustainability while achieving necessary gas efficiency.

15. Memory vs Storage Usage

Memory and storage management in Solidity represents one of the most critical aspects of smart contract development, directly impacting both gas costs and contract performance. Understanding the fundamental differences between memory and storage, along with their optimal usage patterns, is essential for developing efficient and cost effective smart contracts.

Storage in Ethereum represents permanent data that persists between function calls and transactions. Every storage operation in smart contracts comes with significant gas costs, as data must be written to the blockchain. Storage variables are stored in specific slots within the contract's storage space, with each slot capable of holding 32 bytes of data. Understanding how the EVM manages these storage slots is crucial for optimizing storage operations.

Memory, in contrast, is a temporary space that exists only during the execution of a function call. Memory is cleared after each external function call, making it significantly cheaper to use than storage for temporary operations. Memory allocation in Solidity follows specific patterns, with the EVM charging different gas costs based on the size and pattern of memory expansion.

When working with complex data structures, choosing between memory and storage has significant implications. Arrays and strings in storage can be particularly expensive to manipulate, as each operation requires blockchain writes. Converting these to memory for temporary operations can provide substantial gas savings. However, developers must carefully manage memory usage to avoid excessive memory expansion costs.

The storage layout of contract variables significantly impacts gas costs. Variables in storage are stored sequentially starting from position 0, but the compiler optimizes storage by packing multiple small variables into a single 32 byte slot when possible. Understanding this packing mechanism allows developers to organize contract variables efficiently. For example, grouping uint8, uint16, and boolean variables together can result in significant storage savings.

Memory management becomes particularly important when dealing with function parameters and return values. When a function accepts or returns arrays or strings, specifying them as memory rather than storage can significantly reduce gas costs for operations that don't require permanent storage. However, developers must be aware that memory arrays have limitations, such as fixed sizes that cannot be modified after creation.

Storage pointers provide a powerful mechanism for efficient data access but must be used carefully. When working with storage structures or arrays, using storage pointers instead of copying data to memory can save gas. However, improper use of storage pointers can lead to unexpected behavior and potential security vulnerabilities. Understanding the lifetime and scope of storage pointers is crucial for their safe implementation.

Memory allocation patterns in loops require special attention. Creating new memory arrays or strings within loops can lead to excessive memory expansion costs. Instead, preallocating memory arrays and reusing memory space can provide significant gas savings. Careful management of memory allocation patterns in loops is essential for optimizing gas costs in contracts that process large amounts of data.

The interaction between memory and storage becomes particularly complex when dealing with nested data structures. Copying complex storage structures to memory requires careful consideration of gas costs and memory management. Implementing efficient copying patterns and avoiding unnecessary data duplication between memory and storage can significantly improve contract performance.

String handling presents unique challenges in terms of memory and storage usage. Strings in Solidity are dynamically sized arrays of bytes, making them particularly expensive to store and manipulate. Converting between storage and memory strings requires careful consideration of gas costs. Implementing efficient string handling patterns, such as using fixed size byte arrays when possible, can provide substantial gas savings.

Mapping types in Solidity present special considerations for memory and storage usage. Mappings can only exist in storage, not in memory, which impacts how data structures using mappings must be designed. Understanding these limitations and implementing appropriate data access patterns is crucial for efficient contract design.

Assembly level memory and storage operations can provide additional optimization opportunities but require careful implementation. Direct manipulation of memory and storage through assembly can bypass some of Solidity's safety checks and overhead, potentially providing significant gas savings. However, these optimizations must be implemented with extreme care to avoid introducing security vulnerabilities.

Memory management in constructor functions requires special consideration. Data assigned in constructors is written directly to storage, making constructor operations particularly expensive. Optimizing constructor logic and carefully managing initialization patterns can reduce deployment costs and improve contract efficiency.

The relationship between memory and storage becomes particularly important in contracts that implement upgradeability patterns. Storage layouts must be carefully managed to maintain data integrity across upgrades, while memory usage patterns must be designed to work efficiently with proxy delegation patterns.

Error handling patterns must consider memory and storage usage implications. Proper error handling should avoid unnecessary storage operations while maintaining sufficient information for debugging and monitoring. Implementing efficient error handling patterns that balance information preservation with gas costs is crucial for production contracts.

Memory and storage optimization patterns must be balanced against code readability and maintainability. While aggressive optimization can provide significant gas savings, it can also make code more difficult to understand and maintain. Documentation of memory and storage usage patterns becomes particularly important when implementing complex optimizations.

Testing strategies for memory and storage usage require specific approaches. Unit tests should verify both the correctness of memory and storage operations and their gas efficiency. Implementing comprehensive test suites that cover various memory and storage usage patterns helps ensure both functionality and efficiency.

Future considerations for memory and storage usage include potential changes in the Ethereum protocol and EVM implementation. Designing contracts with flexible memory and storage patterns that can adapt to future protocol changes helps ensure long term contract viability. Regular review and updates of memory and storage usage patterns helps maintain optimal contract performance as the ecosystem evolves.

16. Upgradeability Patterns

Upgradeability patterns represent a critical aspect of smart contract development, enabling developers to modify and enhance contract functionality while maintaining data persistence and system stability. As blockchain applications evolve and new requirements emerge, the ability to upgrade smart contracts becomes essential for maintaining secure and efficient decentralized systems.

The fundamental challenge of contract upgradeability stems from the immutable nature of blockchain deployments. Once deployed, a smart contract's code cannot be modified directly. Upgradeability patterns overcome this limitation through carefully designed architectures that separate contract logic from storage while maintaining secure access controls and data integrity.

The most basic upgradeability pattern involves deploying a new contract and migrating data from the old contract. This approach, while straightforward, often proves impractical for complex systems due to high gas costs and potential disruption of service. More sophisticated patterns have emerged to address these limitations, providing seamless upgrades while maintaining system continuity.

The delegate proxy pattern represents one of the most widely adopted upgradeability approaches. In this pattern, a proxy contract maintains the storage state and delegates function calls to an implementation contract containing the logic. Users interact with the proxy contract's address, which remains constant, while the implementation contract can be upgraded by updating the delegation reference. This pattern requires careful consideration of storage layouts and function selector handling.

Storage layouts in upgradeable contracts demand particular attention. The storage structure must remain consistent across upgrades to prevent data corruption. A common approach involves using unstructured storage patterns, where storage slots are assigned using deterministic hashing rather than sequential allocation. This approach prevents storage collisions and allows for more flexible contract evolution.

The transparent proxy pattern extends the basic proxy pattern by addressing function selector clashing issues. This pattern implements specific rules for handling admin functions versus user functions, preventing potential conflicts between proxy and implementation selectors. The transparency comes from clear separation between upgrade administration and normal contract functionality.

Implementation contracts in upgradeable systems must follow specific design patterns. They typically avoid using constructors, instead implementing initializer functions that can be called once after deployment. Storage variables must be declared in a consistent order across versions, and new variables must be appended to maintain compatibility with existing storage layouts.

Version management becomes crucial in upgradeable systems. Implementing clear versioning mechanisms helps track contract iterations and validate upgrade paths. This includes maintaining comprehensive documentation of changes between versions and implementing version checking mechanisms within the contracts themselves.

Access control patterns play a vital role in upgrade security. Implementing robust administrative controls ensures that only authorized entities can perform upgrades. Multi signature requirements and time locks for upgrade operations provide additional security layers, preventing unauthorized or malicious upgrades.

The beacon proxy pattern offers an alternative approach for managing multiple upgradeable contracts. Instead of each proxy maintaining its own implementation reference, they reference a beacon contract that stores the implementation address. This pattern simplifies upgrading multiple contracts simultaneously and reduces gas costs for large scale deployments.

Testing upgradeable contracts requires specific strategies. Tests must verify not only the functionality of individual versions but also the upgrade process itself. This includes testing storage migration, function selector handling, and access control mechanisms. Comprehensive upgrade testing helps prevent potential issues during production deployments.

The diamond pattern represents an advanced upgradeability approach, allowing for modular contract functionality. This pattern enables selective upgrading of specific contract facets while maintaining others, providing greater flexibility in system evolution. However, the increased complexity requires careful implementation and thorough testing.

Error handling in upgradeable contracts must account for potential version mismatches and upgrade failures. Implementing robust fallback mechanisms and error recovery procedures helps maintain system stability during and after upgrades. Clear error messages and event logging facilitate debugging and monitoring of upgrade processes.

Gas optimization remains important in upgradeable contracts, particularly considering the additional overhead of delegation calls. Carefully designed storage layouts and efficient function implementations help minimize gas costs while maintaining upgradeability. Regular gas usage analysis across contract versions helps identify potential optimization opportunities.

Security considerations for upgradeable contracts extend beyond standard smart contract vulnerabilities. Developers must carefully consider potential attack vectors related to the upgrade process itself, including front running attacks on upgrades and potential storage manipulation through deprecated functions. Regular security audits of both implementation contracts and upgrade mechanisms help maintain system security.

Documentation plays a crucial role in managing upgradeable contracts. Maintaining detailed records of storage layouts, function signatures, and upgrade procedures helps ensure successful upgrades and system maintenance. Clear documentation of upgrade policies and procedures supports both development teams and contract administrators.

Future proofing upgrade mechanisms requires consideration of potential protocol changes and evolving security requirements. Designing flexible upgrade patterns that can adapt to new requirements while maintaining backward compatibility helps ensure long term system viability. Regular review and updates of upgrade mechanisms help maintain system security and efficiency.

The implementation of upgradeability patterns must balance flexibility with security and efficiency. While upgradeability provides valuable benefits for contract maintenance and evolution, it also introduces additional complexity and potential security risks. Careful consideration of system requirements and thorough implementation of security measures helps create robust upgradeable systems.

17. Proxy Contracts Implementation

In smart contract development, proxy contracts serve as a fundamental building block for implementing upgradeability patterns. This chapter delves deep into the practical implementation of proxy contracts, exploring various approaches and best practices for creating robust, secure, and maintainable upgradeable systems.

The core concept of proxy contract implementation revolves around the separation of concerns between contract storage and logic. A proxy contract maintains the storage state and delegates function calls to an implementation contract that contains the business logic. This separation enables upgrades by pointing the proxy to new implementation contracts while preserving the storage state.

Implementing a basic proxy contract requires careful consideration of several key components. The proxy must include a storage slot for the implementation address, delegation logic for forwarding calls, and secure mechanisms for upgrading the implementation reference. Here's an examination of these essential elements and their implementation details.

The storage slot for the implementation address typically uses a specific pattern to avoid storage collisions. Rather than using a simple storage variable, many implementations use assembly to store the implementation address at a predetermined slot. This approach ensures consistent storage layouts across upgrades and prevents potential conflicts with implementation contract storage.

Delegation logic forms the heart of proxy contract implementation. The proxy uses assembly level operations to forward calls to the implementation contract while maintaining the original caller's context. This involves careful handling of calldata, return data, and revert messages to ensure transparent delegation of function calls.

Access control mechanisms in proxy contracts must be robust and secure. Implementation of access controls typically involves specific storage slots for admin addresses and carefully designed upgrade functions. Many implementations include time locks or multi signature requirements for upgrade operations to enhance security.

The implementation of function selector handling requires particular attention. Proxy contracts must correctly distinguish between administrative functions (handled by the proxy itself) and delegated functions (forwarded to the implementation). This distinction prevents function selector clashing and ensures proper handling of all contract interactions.

Storage patterns in proxy implementations demand careful consideration. Many implementations use unstructured storage approaches, where storage slots are calculated using keccak256 hashes of specific identifiers. This pattern prevents storage collisions and provides flexibility for storage layout evolution across upgrades.

Initialization patterns play a crucial role in proxy contract implementation. Since constructors cannot be used in implementation contracts (as they're not included in the deployed bytecode), initialization functions must be carefully implemented and protected against multiple initialization attempts.

Event logging in proxy contracts helps track important system changes and facilitates monitoring. Implementation should include events for upgrades, administrative changes, and other significant operations. Proper event implementation supports system transparency and aids in debugging and monitoring.

Error handling in proxy implementations must account for various failure scenarios. This includes handling delegation failures, implementation contract errors, and administrative operation failures. Clear error messages and proper error propagation help maintain system reliability and facilitate troubleshooting.

Gas optimization in proxy implementations requires careful balance between functionality and efficiency. While delegation adds some overhead, various optimization techniques can minimize gas costs. This includes efficient storage layouts, optimized assembly operations, and careful consideration of function parameters.

Implementation of proxy contracts often includes version management mechanisms. This involves storing version information, implementing version checks, and maintaining upgrade paths. Proper version management helps ensure system consistency and facilitates maintenance operations.

Security considerations in proxy implementation extend beyond basic access controls. Implementations must guard against potential attacks such as storage collision attacks, initialization front running, and implementation contract manipulation. Regular security reviews and comprehensive testing help maintain system security.

Testing proxy implementations requires specific approaches. Tests must cover both the proxy contract functionality and the upgrade mechanisms. This includes testing delegation paths, access controls, storage patterns, and upgrade procedures. Comprehensive testing helps ensure reliable system operation.

Documentation of proxy implementations must be thorough and clear. This includes detailed documentation of storage layouts, function selectors, initialization procedures, and upgrade mechanisms. Clear documentation supports both development teams and system administrators in maintaining the system.

Integration with external systems requires careful consideration in proxy implementations. This includes handling external contract interactions, maintaining interface compatibility, and managing dependencies. Proper integration patterns help ensure system interoperability and maintainability.

Future proofing proxy implementations involves considering potential protocol changes and evolving requirements. This includes designing flexible upgrade mechanisms, maintaining backward compatibility, and planning for potential protocol upgrades. Regular review and updates help maintain system viability.

Monitoring and maintenance procedures for proxy implementations must be well defined. This includes implementing monitoring systems, establishing maintenance procedures, and defining incident response protocols. Proper maintenance procedures help ensure long term system reliability.

The implementation of proxy contracts represents a critical aspect of creating upgradeable smart contract systems. Success requires careful attention to detail, thorough testing, and comprehensive security measures. When properly implemented, proxy contracts provide a powerful foundation for building flexible and maintainable blockchain applications.

18. Diamond Pattern for Complex Systems

The Diamond Pattern represents a sophisticated evolution in smart contract architecture, particularly suited for complex systems that require modularity, upgradeability, and efficient gas usage. Unlike traditional proxy patterns, the Diamond Pattern allows for multiple implementation contracts to be managed through a single proxy, offering unprecedented flexibility in contract organization and maintenance.

At its core, the Diamond Pattern introduces the concept of facets, which are implementation contracts containing related functionality. These facets are managed through a central diamond contract that serves as the entry point for all interactions. This architecture allows developers to organize complex systems into logical components while maintaining a unified interface for users.

The implementation of the Diamond Pattern begins with the diamond contract itself. This contract maintains a mapping of function selectors to their corresponding facet addresses, enabling precise control over which functions are delegated to which implementation contracts. The diamond contract also implements core diamond functionality, including mechanisms for adding, replacing, and removing facets.

Storage management in the Diamond Pattern requires careful consideration. The pattern typically employs the Diamond Storage pattern, where each facet defines its own storage structure using a specific storage slot derived from a unique identifier. This approach prevents storage collisions between facets while maintaining upgrade flexibility. Implementation requires careful coordination of storage layouts across all facets to ensure data integrity.

Function delegation in the Diamond Pattern involves sophisticated selector management. When a function call arrives at the diamond contract, it must efficiently determine which facet handles the called function and delegate the call appropriately. This process requires optimized lookup mechanisms to minimize gas costs while maintaining system reliability. Implementation typically involves assembly level operations for efficient delegation.

The Diamond Pattern introduces the concept of diamond cuts, which are atomic operations that modify the facet configuration of a diamond. A diamond cut can add new facets, replace existing ones, or remove facets entirely. Implementation of diamond cuts must ensure atomicity and maintain system consistency throughout the modification process. This includes proper validation of new facets and careful handling of storage during upgrades.

Access control in Diamond Pattern implementations requires comprehensive security measures. The pattern typically implements role based access control for managing diamond cuts and administrative functions. Implementation must include secure role management, careful permission validation, and proper event logging for all administrative actions.

Event logging plays a crucial role in Diamond Pattern implementations. The pattern defines specific events for diamond cuts, facet changes, and other significant system operations. Proper implementation of events ensures system transparency and facilitates monitoring and debugging of diamond operations.

Gas optimization becomes particularly important in Diamond Pattern implementations due to the additional complexity of function delegation. Implementation must balance the flexibility of the pattern with efficient execution. This includes optimizing selector lookup mechanisms, minimizing storage operations, and carefully managing delegation overhead.

Initialization patterns in Diamond Pattern implementations require special attention. Since facets cannot use constructors, initialization must be handled through specific initialization functions.

Implementation must ensure proper initialization sequencing and prevent unauthorized or duplicate initialization attempts.

Version management in Diamond Pattern implementations involves tracking both individual facet versions and overall diamond configurations. Implementation typically includes version tracking mechanisms, upgrade path validation, and configuration management tools. This supports system maintenance and ensures consistent upgrades.

Testing Diamond Pattern implementations requires comprehensive approaches covering multiple aspects. Tests must verify individual facet functionality, diamond cut operations, storage integrity, and system wide behavior. Implementation of testing frameworks must account for the distributed nature of functionality across facets.

Documentation of Diamond Pattern implementations must be particularly thorough due to the system's complexity. This includes detailed documentation of facet interfaces, storage layouts, diamond cut specifications, and upgrade procedures. Clear documentation supports both development teams and system administrators.

Error handling in Diamond Pattern implementations must account for various failure scenarios across multiple facets. Implementation includes proper error propagation, clear error messages, and robust recovery mechanisms. This ensures system reliability and facilitates troubleshooting.

Integration with external systems in Diamond Pattern implementations requires careful consideration of interface compatibility and dependency management. Implementation must ensure consistent behavior across facets when interacting with external contracts while maintaining system modularity.

Monitoring and maintenance procedures for Diamond Pattern implementations must be comprehensive. This includes implementing monitoring systems for individual facets and overall system health, establishing maintenance procedures, and defining incident response protocols. Proper maintenance procedures ensure long term system reliability.

The Diamond Pattern represents a powerful tool for managing complex smart contract systems. Its implementation requires careful attention to detail, thorough understanding of system requirements, and comprehensive security measures. When properly implemented, the Diamond Pattern provides a robust foundation for building sophisticated, maintainable blockchain applications that can evolve over time while maintaining security and efficiency.

19. Event Logging and Monitoring

Event logging and monitoring are fundamental aspects of smart contract development that provide transparency, facilitate debugging, and enable effective system oversight. When implemented properly, events serve as an immutable audit trail of contract activities and provide essential data for both developers and users of decentralized applications.

Events in Solidity are declared using the event keyword and can include both indexed and non-indexed parameters. Indexed parameters, limited to a maximum of three per event, create topics that can be efficiently queried from the blockchain. The implementation of events requires careful consideration of gas costs, as each logged event consumes gas proportional to the amount of data being stored.

A comprehensive event logging strategy begins with identifying key contract actions that warrant event emission. These typically include state changes, administrative actions, financial transactions, and security-related events. When implementing events, developers should strike a balance between logging sufficient information for transparency and monitoring while avoiding excessive gas costs from logging unnecessary data.

The proper structuring of event parameters is crucial for effective monitoring. Indexed parameters should be chosen based on their utility for filtering and querying events. Common patterns include indexing addresses for sender and receiver tracking, function selectors for operation identification, and unique identifiers for specific transactions or entities. Non-indexed parameters can store additional context that might be needed for detailed analysis but doesn't require direct querying.

Implementation of event logging should follow consistent patterns across the contract system. This includes standardized naming conventions, parameter ordering, and documentation of event purposes. A common pattern is to prefix events with the contract name or module identifier to prevent confusion in complex systems with multiple contracts emitting similar events.

Monitoring systems built around smart contract events require robust infrastructure for capturing and processing event data. Implementation typically involves setting up event listeners that connect to Ethereum nodes, process incoming events, and store relevant data in more accessible formats. This infrastructure must handle network issues, chain reorganizations, and high event volumes while maintaining data consistency.

Event monitoring systems should implement alert mechanisms for critical events. These alerts can be triggered by specific event signatures, parameter values, or patterns of activity. Implementation requires careful threshold setting and alert routing to prevent alert fatigue while ensuring important events receive appropriate attention.

Security events deserve special consideration in the logging implementation. Critical security-related events such as ownership transfers, permission changes, or emergency stops should always be logged. These events should include sufficient context to understand the security impact and facilitate incident response when necessary.

Monitoring systems should implement data aggregation and analysis capabilities. This includes tracking metrics like transaction volumes, gas usage patterns, and user activity. Implementation often involves time-series databases and analytics tools that can process event data to generate insights about contract usage and performance.

Historical event analysis capabilities are essential for debugging and auditing. Implementation should include tools for efficiently querying historical events, reconstructing state changes, and validating system behavior over time. This requires careful consideration of data storage and indexing strategies to maintain quick access to historical event data.

Real-time monitoring implementations must handle the inherent latency of blockchain networks. This includes accounting for block confirmation times, managing pending transactions, and handling chain reorganizations. Implementation patterns typically include buffer periods for event finality and mechanisms to detect and correct for chain reorganizations.

Event replay capabilities are valuable for system testing and state verification. Implementation should support replaying historical events to validate system behavior or reconstruct state. This requires careful event design to ensure all necessary information for state reconstruction is included in event parameters.

Performance monitoring through events requires careful implementation of metrics collection. This includes logging gas usage patterns, function call frequencies, and timing information. Implementation should balance the granularity of performance data collection with the associated gas costs.

User activity monitoring through events supports both security and usability analysis. Implementation should include events that track user interactions, enabling analysis of usage patterns and detection of potential security issues. This requires careful consideration of privacy implications and regulatory requirements regarding user data collection.

Integration with external monitoring systems requires standardized event formats and reliable data delivery mechanisms. Implementation typically involves building adapters that transform blockchain events into formats compatible with existing monitoring infrastructure. This ensures seamless integration with organizational security and operations tools.

Fault detection systems built on event monitoring require sophisticated pattern recognition capabilities. Implementation should include mechanisms for detecting anomalous patterns of events that might indicate system issues or security threats. This requires careful tuning of detection algorithms to minimize false positives while catching genuine issues.

Event logging and monitoring implementations must consider gas optimization strategies. This includes batching related events when possible, carefully choosing between indexed and non-indexed parameters, and potentially implementing filtering mechanisms at the contract level to reduce unnecessary event emissions.

Documentation of event logging implementations should be comprehensive and include detailed descriptions of each event's purpose, parameters, and expected usage. This documentation supports both development teams and external integrators in effectively utilizing the event logging system.

Testing event logging implementations requires verification of both event emission and monitoring system functionality. This includes testing event parameter accuracy, monitoring system reliability, and alert mechanism effectiveness. Comprehensive testing ensures the logging and monitoring system provides reliable oversight of contract operations.

20. External Contract Interactions

External contract interactions are a critical aspect of smart contract development that require careful consideration of security implications and potential vulnerabilities. Smart contracts frequently need to interact with other contracts on the blockchain, whether calling functions, transferring tokens, or integrating with established protocols. Understanding how to implement these interactions safely is essential for building secure decentralized applications.

The fundamental pattern for external contract interactions involves using interface definitions to establish type-safe communication channels between contracts. Interfaces define the function signatures that can be called on the target contract, enabling compile-time checking of parameter types and return values. When implementing external calls, developers should always use explicit interface definitions rather than low-level calls to ensure proper type checking and function signature verification.

One of the primary security considerations when implementing external contract interactions is the potential for reentrancy attacks. When calling external contracts, the called contract can execute arbitrary code, including making callbacks to the original contract before the first call completes. Secure implementation requires following the checks-effects-interactions pattern, where all state changes are completed before making external calls, and using reentrancy guards when necessary.

Address validation is crucial when implementing external contract interactions. Before making any external calls, contracts should verify that the target address is valid and contains code. This can be accomplished using the isContract function or similar checks. Additionally, implementations should include mechanisms to update target contract addresses when necessary, particularly in upgradeable systems.

Error handling in external contract interactions requires careful consideration. Failed external calls can occur for various reasons, including out-of-gas conditions, reverted transactions, or non-existent functions. Implementation should include proper error handling mechanisms, such as try/catch blocks for external calls, and appropriate fallback behavior when calls fail.

Gas forwarding patterns must be considered when implementing external contract interactions. When making external calls that require gas, implementations should carefully manage gas forwarding to ensure sufficient gas is available for the called function while preventing potential denial of service attacks through excessive gas consumption.

Return value handling from external calls requires careful implementation. Some older contracts may not return values consistently, and different token standards handle returns differently. Implementation should include proper checking of return values and fallback mechanisms when expected returns are not received.

Callback patterns in external contract interactions need secure implementation. When contracts implement callback functions that will be called by external contracts, careful consideration must be given to access control, state management, and potential reentrancy vectors. Implementation should include proper validation of callback sources and protection against malicious callbacks.

Token interaction patterns require special attention in implementation. When interacting with token contracts, implementations should follow established patterns for approval and transfer functions, including checking return values and implementing proper allowance management. This includes handling both standard and non-standard token implementations safely.

Version compatibility must be considered when implementing external contract interactions. Different contract versions may have different function signatures or behavior. Implementation should include version checking mechanisms and fallback options for handling different contract versions safely.

Batched interaction patterns can improve efficiency but require careful implementation. When multiple external calls are needed, batching them can reduce gas costs and improve atomicity. However, implementation must consider the potential for partial execution and include proper rollback mechanisms when necessary.

Proxy contract interactions require special handling in implementation. When interacting with proxy contracts, implementations should account for potential delegation and upgrade patterns, ensuring calls are properly routed to the current implementation contract.

Security considerations for external contract interactions include protecting against malicious contracts. Implementation should include mechanisms to validate contract behavior, limit exposure to untrusted contracts, and implement circuit breakers for critical interactions.

Monitoring external contract interactions is essential for security and maintenance. Implementation should include comprehensive event logging for external calls, including success and failure states, gas usage, and relevant parameters for debugging and auditing.

Testing external contract interactions requires comprehensive scenarios. Implementation of test suites should include mocking external contracts, simulating various failure modes, and validating behavior under different network conditions.

Contract composition patterns must be carefully considered when implementing external interactions. When contracts depend on multiple external contracts, implementation should manage these dependencies carefully, including proper initialization order and handling of circular dependencies.

Rate limiting and throttling mechanisms may be necessary for external interactions. Implementation should include mechanisms to prevent excessive calls to external contracts, protecting against potential denial of service attacks and managing gas costs effectively.

Documentation of external contract interactions should be comprehensive. Implementation details, including expected behavior, error handling, and security considerations, should be clearly documented to support maintenance and auditing.

The implementation of external contract interactions must consider the potential for front-running and transaction ordering attacks. This includes implementing appropriate protection mechanisms such as commit-reveal schemes or maximum slippage parameters where necessary.

Finally, upgradeability considerations must be addressed in external interaction implementation. As external contracts may be upgraded or deprecated, implementation should include mechanisms to handle contract upgrades and maintain system functionality across changes in external dependencies.

21. Safe Token Implementation

Safe token implementation is a fundamental aspect of smart contract development that requires careful attention to security, functionality, and efficiency. When implementing tokens on the Ethereum blockchain, developers must consider various aspects including standard compliance, secure transfer mechanisms, proper access controls, and protection against common vulnerabilities.

The foundation of safe token implementation begins with understanding and correctly implementing token standards. While ERC20 remains the most widely used token standard, implementations must go beyond the basic interface requirements to ensure security. A secure token implementation should include comprehensive safeguards against common attack vectors while maintaining compatibility with existing infrastructure.

Access control mechanisms form a critical component of safe token implementation. Token contracts should implement clear ownership and administrative functions with appropriate access restrictions. This includes functions for minting, burning, pausing, and upgrading token functionality. Implementation should utilize well tested access control patterns such as OpenZeppelin's Ownable or Role Based Access Control (RBAC) systems.

Transfer mechanisms require particular attention in token implementation. The transfer and transferFrom functions should include comprehensive checks for zero addresses, sufficient balances, and proper allowance management. Implementations should also consider the implications of transfer fees, reflection mechanisms, or other custom transfer logic while ensuring these do not introduce vulnerabilities.

Safe token implementation must include protection against integer overflow and underflow vulnerabilities. While newer versions of Solidity include automatic checks, explicit safeguards should still be implemented, particularly when dealing with custom mathematical operations. This includes using safe math libraries or implementing checked arithmetic operations.

Events play a crucial role in token implementation. Proper event emission ensures transparency and enables external systems to track token movements and state changes. Implementation should include comprehensive event logging for all significant state changes, including transfers, approvals, and administrative actions.

Token supply management requires secure implementation. Whether implementing a fixed supply or dynamic supply token, the mechanisms for managing total supply must be carefully controlled. This includes proper tracking of minted and burned tokens, and protection against supply manipulation attacks.

Approval mechanisms in token implementation require careful consideration. The standard approve and transferFrom pattern can be vulnerable to certain attacks. Secure implementations should consider using increase/decrease allowance functions instead of simple approve, and implement proper checks against allowance manipulation.

Batch operation support in token implementation can improve efficiency but requires careful implementation. When implementing batch transfers or approvals, proper validation of all operations must be performed before any state changes occur. Implementation should also consider gas limitations and potential partial execution scenarios.

Pausability may be required in token implementation for emergency situations. If implemented, pause mechanisms should be carefully controlled and include proper access restrictions. Implementation should consider the implications of pausing on various token functions and include appropriate events and state tracking.

Upgradeability patterns may be necessary in token implementation to allow for future improvements or bug fixes. If upgradeability is required, implementation should follow established patterns such as proxy contracts while ensuring proper initialization and state management across upgrades.

Blacklist and whitelist functionality may be necessary for regulatory compliance or security purposes. If implemented, these mechanisms should include proper access controls and clear documentation of criteria for address restriction. Implementation should consider the implications on transfer mechanisms and include appropriate events.

Gas optimization is crucial in token implementation, particularly for tokens expected to have high transaction volumes. Implementation should optimize storage usage, minimize redundant computations, and consider batch operations where appropriate while maintaining security requirements.

Token burning mechanisms require secure implementation. If token burning is supported, implementation should include proper validation of burn amounts, clear tracking of burned tokens, and appropriate events. The relationship between burning and total supply must be carefully managed.

Recovery mechanisms may be necessary in token implementation to handle tokens accidentally sent to the contract address. Implementation should include secure methods for recovering various token types while maintaining proper access controls and avoiding potential vulnerabilities.

Metadata management in token implementation requires consideration. If the token includes metadata such as name, symbol, or decimals, implementation should include proper initialization and, if needed, secure update mechanisms with appropriate access controls.

Rate limiting mechanisms may be necessary in token implementation to prevent abuse or meet regulatory requirements. Implementation should consider adding transfer limits, cooling periods, or other rate limiting mechanisms while ensuring these do not introduce vulnerabilities.

Integration with external contracts requires careful consideration in token implementation. When implementing functionality that interacts with other contracts, proper validation and security measures must be in place to prevent potential attacks or unexpected behavior.

Testing requirements for token implementation are extensive. Implementation should include comprehensive test coverage for all functions, including edge cases, error conditions, and potential attack vectors. This includes unit tests, integration tests, and specific security focused tests.

Documentation of token implementation should be thorough and clear. This includes detailed specifications of all functions, events, and state variables, as well as clear documentation of any custom features or security considerations. Implementation details should be well commented and include rationale for security critical decisions.

Audit preparation is essential in token implementation. The implementation should follow best practices for code organization, include comprehensive documentation, and address common audit findings proactively. This includes clear specification of trust assumptions and security models.

22. ERC Standards Security

ERC standards security is a critical aspect of smart contract development that requires meticulous attention to detail and comprehensive understanding of the established token standards. These standards, developed through Ethereum Improvement Proposals (EIPs), provide frameworks for implementing tokens with consistent interfaces and behaviors. However, merely following these standards is not enough; developers must understand and implement additional security measures to protect against various vulnerabilities and attack vectors.

The ERC20 standard, while widely adopted, contains several potential security pitfalls that developers must address. One of the most notable issues is the approve/transferFrom race condition, where an attacker can potentially spend more tokens than intended by front running approval transactions. To mitigate this, implementations should use increaseAllowance and decreaseAllowance functions instead of the basic approve function, allowing for atomic updates to allowances.

Another critical consideration in ERC20 implementation is the handling of zero address transfers. The standard does not explicitly require checking for zero addresses, but secure implementations should include these checks to prevent accidental token burning. Similarly, proper validation of input parameters, especially in transfer and transferFrom functions, is essential to prevent unintended behavior or token loss.

The ERC721 standard for non fungible tokens presents its own set of security challenges. Proper implementation must include checks for valid token ownership before transfers, accurate tracking of token existence, and protection against double transfers. The standard's transfer mechanics, particularly the safeTransfer functions, must be carefully implemented to handle receiver contracts correctly and prevent tokens from being locked in contracts that cannot handle them.

ERC1155's multi token standard combines features of both fungible and non fungible tokens, making security considerations more complex. Implementations must carefully handle batch operations, ensuring atomicity and proper validation of all transfers in a batch. The standard's hook functions, particularly onERC1155Received and onERC1155BatchReceived, must be properly implemented to prevent tokens from being locked in contracts.

Security considerations for metadata handling in token standards are often overlooked. For ERC721 and ERC1155 tokens, the URI functionality must be implemented securely, ensuring that metadata links cannot be maliciously modified and that the metadata itself is properly protected. Implementations should consider using immutable or controlled upgrade patterns for metadata management.

Interface detection is another crucial security aspect across all ERC standards. Proper implementation of supportsInterface is essential for contract interoperability and preventing interface related vulnerabilities. Implementations should accurately report supported interfaces and include proper validation when interacting with other contracts.

The ERC777 standard, designed as an improvement over ERC20, introduces hooks for sending and receiving tokens. While these hooks provide additional functionality, they also introduce potential reentrancy vulnerabilities. Implementations must carefully handle these hooks, ensuring proper checks and balances are in place to prevent malicious exploitation.

Token burning mechanisms across different standards require careful implementation. Whether implementing ERC20, ERC721, or ERC1155 tokens, burning functions must properly update total supply tracking, emit appropriate events, and ensure tokens cannot be accidentally or maliciously burned without proper authorization.

Access control patterns in ERC standard implementations must be carefully considered. While the standards themselves don't mandate specific access control mechanisms, secure implementations should include proper role based access control for administrative functions such as minting, pausing, or upgrading functionality.

Gas optimization in ERC standard implementations requires balance between efficiency and security. While optimizing gas usage is important, particularly for high volume tokens, implementations must not sacrifice security measures for gas savings. This includes maintaining proper checks and validations while optimizing storage patterns and computation.

Event emission across ERC standards must be properly implemented for transparency and tracking. All significant state changes should emit appropriate events, following the standard specifications while potentially including additional events for custom functionality or enhanced tracking capabilities.

The implementation of approval mechanisms across different standards requires careful consideration of potential attack vectors. This includes proper handling of approvals for operators in ERC721 and ERC1155, and careful implementation of approval inheritance in proxy contract patterns.

Upgradeability patterns for ERC standard implementations must maintain standard compliance across upgrades. This includes proper handling of storage layouts, initialization of new functionality, and maintaining consistent interfaces while adding security improvements or new features.

Recovery mechanisms for tokens sent directly to contract addresses must be carefully implemented across all standards. This includes proper handling of both native token recovery and recovery of other token types that might be accidentally sent to the contract.

Integration with external contracts and protocols requires careful consideration of standard compliance and security. Implementations should include proper validation of external contract interactions, especially when implementing hooks or callback functions defined in the standards.

Testing requirements for ERC standard implementations must be comprehensive, covering all standard functions and additional security features. This includes testing for compliance with the standard specifications, edge cases, and potential attack vectors specific to each standard.

Documentation for ERC standard implementations should clearly specify any deviations from or additions to the standard specifications. This includes detailed documentation of security measures, custom functionality, and rationale for implementation choices.

Audit preparation for ERC standard implementations should include comprehensive testing of standard compliance along with security measures. This includes clear documentation of trust assumptions, security models, and any custom functionality beyond the standard specifications.

The evolution of ERC standards continues to introduce new security considerations and best practices. Developers must stay informed about updates to standards, new security findings, and emerging best practices while maintaining backward compatibility and security in their implementations.

23. Randomness in Smart Contracts

Randomness in smart contracts presents one of the most challenging aspects of secure blockchain development. While deterministic execution is a fundamental feature of blockchain technology, many decentralized applications require some form of randomness for various purposes, from gaming applications to fair selection processes. Understanding how to implement secure randomness while avoiding common pitfalls is crucial for smart contract developers.

The primary challenge with randomness in smart contracts stems from the deterministic nature of the Ethereum Virtual Machine. Every node in the network must be able to execute the same code and arrive at the same result. This makes true randomness impossible to achieve purely on chain, as any seemingly random value must be derived from data available to all nodes.

Common misconceptions about randomness often lead developers to implement insecure solutions. Using block variables such as block.timestamp or block.difficulty as sources of randomness is particularly dangerous. These values can be manipulated by miners to some degree, making them unsuitable for applications where the randomness needs to be truly unpredictable and fair.

The block.timestamp, while appearing random to casual observers, can be manipulated by miners within a certain range. Miners can adjust the timestamp within about 15 seconds of the actual time, potentially allowing them to influence outcomes that depend on this value. Similarly, block.difficulty can be manipulated through selective mining strategies, making it an unreliable source of randomness.

A more secure approach to generating random numbers involves using a commit reveal scheme. In this pattern, participants first commit to a hidden value (typically a hash of their chosen number plus some secret), and then reveal their values in a subsequent phase. The final random number is derived from the combination of all revealed values. This approach provides better unpredictability, as no single participant can determine the final outcome without knowing all other participants' values.

Chainlink VRF (Verifiable Random Function) has emerged as a leading solution for secure randomness in smart contracts. It provides cryptographically guaranteed randomness that can be verified on chain. The VRF service works by combining a seed provided by the requesting contract with the oracle's secret key to generate both a random number and a cryptographic proof. The proof can be verified on chain to ensure the randomness was generated correctly and wasn't manipulated.

When implementing randomness in smart contracts, developers must carefully consider the timing of random number generation and result consumption. A common vulnerability occurs when the random number generation and its usage are not properly separated, allowing observers to predict outcomes or manipulate results. This is particularly important in gaming applications where large amounts of value might be at stake.

Multi block randomness generation can provide additional security by deriving randomness from multiple block variables across several blocks. This approach makes it more difficult for miners to manipulate the outcome, as they would need to control multiple consecutive blocks. However, this method introduces latency into the random number generation process and may not be suitable for applications requiring immediate results.

Future block randomness, while seemingly secure, can be vulnerable to manipulation through transaction ordering. Miners can choose whether to include certain transactions based on how they affect the randomness outcome. Therefore, developers should avoid relying on future block values for randomness generation unless additional security measures are in place.

Entropy pools offer another approach to generating randomness by accumulating multiple sources of pseudo random data over time. These pools can combine user provided values, transaction hashes, block variables, and other sources of entropy. While this approach can provide better randomness than single source solutions, careful implementation is required to prevent manipulation of the pool contents.

Gas considerations play an important role in randomness implementation. Complex random number generation schemes can consume significant gas, making them impractical for certain applications. Developers must balance security requirements with gas efficiency, potentially implementing off chain components where appropriate while maintaining verifiability on chain.

Error handling in random number generation requires special attention. Failed random number generation should not leave the contract in an inconsistent state or allow participants to gain unfair advantages. Proper error handling mechanisms should be implemented to handle cases where randomness generation fails or is delayed.

Testing randomness implementations presents unique challenges due to the deterministic nature of test environments. Developers should implement comprehensive testing strategies that include simulation of various attack scenarios and verification of the statistical properties of the generated random numbers.

When implementing random number generation for high value applications, consider using multiple sources of randomness combined in a secure way. This could include external oracles, commit reveal schemes, and on chain entropy sources. The combination of multiple sources can provide better security than relying on any single source.

Monitoring and alerting systems should be implemented to detect potential manipulation attempts or unusual patterns in random number generation. This includes monitoring for suspicious transaction patterns, unusual timing of reveals in commit reveal schemes, and unexpected statistical distributions in the generated numbers.

Documentation of randomness implementation should clearly specify the security assumptions, limitations, and potential vulnerabilities of the chosen approach. Users of the system should understand the level of randomness guaranteed and any timing constraints or other limitations that might affect their use of the system.

The future of randomness in smart contracts may see new solutions emerging, particularly with the development of zero knowledge proofs and other cryptographic techniques. Developers should stay informed about new developments in this space while maintaining a careful approach to implementing randomness in their current applications.

24. Time-Based Contract Logic

Time-based contract logic is a fundamental aspect of many smart contracts, enabling functionality that depends on temporal conditions and scheduling. However, implementing time-based operations securely requires careful consideration of blockchain mechanics and potential attack vectors.

Smart contracts commonly need to handle time-dependent operations such as token vesting schedules, time-locked wallets, auction deadlines, governance voting periods, and interest calculations. The primary mechanism for implementing time-based logic in Solidity is through block timestamps, accessed via block.timestamp or its alias now. While these provide a way to reference time, developers must understand their limitations and security implications.

Block timestamps in Ethereum are not perfectly precise. Miners have some flexibility in setting the timestamp, typically within a range of about 15 seconds. While this might seem insignificant, it can become crucial in contracts where precise timing is essential or where significant value depends on exact timestamp comparisons. Developers should build in appropriate buffer periods and avoid requiring exact timestamp matches in their contract logic.

When implementing time locks or vesting schedules, it's important to use relative time calculations rather than absolute timestamps whenever possible. Instead of storing specific target timestamps, store the duration or the time difference required. This approach makes the contract more resilient to deployment delays and easier to test. For example, rather than setting a specific unlock date, store the required lock duration and calculate the unlock time relative to the deployment or initialization timestamp.

Time-based state transitions require careful implementation to prevent race conditions and ensure consistent contract state. Consider a contract that needs to transition through different phases based on time. The transition logic should be implemented in a way that ensures state changes occur deterministically and cannot be manipulated by transaction ordering. One pattern is to implement a state check function that updates the contract state based on the current timestamp before executing time-sensitive operations.

Duration calculations in smart contracts should account for potential edge cases and overflow scenarios. When working with timestamps, which are typically large numbers, arithmetic operations can potentially overflow. Using SafeMath or Solidity 0.8.x's built-in overflow checking is essential. Additionally, developers should be mindful of the limitations of uint256 when calculating far future timestamps or long durations.

Implementing cooldown periods or rate limiting requires careful consideration of timestamp manipulation. While minor timestamp manipulation by miners is possible, properly implemented cooldown mechanisms can still effectively prevent rapid repeated actions. The key is to ensure the cooldown period is significantly longer than the potential timestamp manipulation window. For critical operations, consider implementing additional security measures beyond simple time-based restrictions.

Time-based access control presents unique challenges. Contracts that grant or revoke permissions based on time must ensure that permission changes are atomic and cannot be circumvented through transaction ordering attacks. Implement clear permission boundaries and ensure that time-based permission changes are properly enforced across all relevant contract functions.

When dealing with recurring time-based events, such as periodic interest payments or reward distributions, careful attention must be paid to accumulation calculations. Floating point arithmetic is not available in Solidity, so time-based calculations often require careful scaling and rounding strategies. Consider implementing checkpoint mechanisms to track accumulated values at specific timestamps rather than performing complex time-based calculations on demand.

Time-based oracle interactions require special consideration. When integrating with external time sources or oracles, implement proper validation and fallback mechanisms. Consider the implications of oracle failures or delays on your time-based logic. Implement appropriate timeout and recovery mechanisms for oracle-dependent operations.

Testing time-based contract logic presents unique challenges. Time manipulation in test environments is essential for thorough testing. Most testing frameworks provide mechanisms to manipulate the blockchain timestamp, allowing developers to simulate the passage of time and test various scenarios. Implement comprehensive tests that cover edge cases around time boundaries and state transitions.

Gas optimization becomes particularly important in contracts with frequent time-based calculations. Cache time-dependent values where appropriate rather than recalculating them frequently. Consider implementing batch processing for periodic operations to distribute gas costs more efficiently. However, ensure that optimization efforts don't compromise the security of time-based logic.

Error handling in time-based operations should be robust and predictable. Implement clear error messages for time-related conditions and ensure that failed time-based operations leave the contract in a consistent state. Consider implementing recovery mechanisms for scenarios where time-based operations fail or become stuck.

Contract upgrades involving time-based logic require special attention. When upgrading contracts with ongoing time-based operations, ensure that temporal state and calculations are properly migrated. Consider implementing version tracking for time-based calculations to maintain backward compatibility where necessary.

Monitoring systems for time-based contracts should track temporal patterns and anomalies. Implement alerts for unexpected time-based state changes or unusual patterns in timestamp-dependent operations. Consider implementing emergency pause mechanisms that can be triggered if time-based operations behave unexpectedly.

Documentation for time-based contract logic should clearly specify timing assumptions and limitations. Users should understand how time is measured and enforced within the contract, including any potential variations or limitations in timestamp accuracy. Document any time-based restrictions or requirements clearly in the contract interface.

The future of time-based contract logic may evolve with new Ethereum improvements and layer 2 solutions. Developers should stay informed about new capabilities and best practices while maintaining robust and secure time-based implementations in their current contracts. Consider the implications of cross-chain operations and different blockchain timing mechanisms when designing time-based logic for modern decentralized applications.

25. Emergency Stop Patterns

Emergency stop patterns, often called circuit breakers or pause mechanisms, are critical safety features in smart contracts that allow operators to halt contract functionality in case of emergencies. These patterns serve as last resort safeguards against potential security incidents, bugs, or unexpected behavior that could put user funds or contract integrity at risk.

The fundamental concept behind emergency stop patterns is to implement a mechanism that can quickly disable critical contract functionality while maintaining essential operations like withdrawals. This capability is particularly important in production environments where contracts manage significant value or complex interactions that could be exploited by malicious actors.

A basic emergency stop implementation typically involves a boolean state variable that tracks whether the contract is paused, along with modifier functions that gate access to sensitive operations. However, sophisticated implementations often require more nuanced approaches that consider various operational states and permission levels. The key is to balance security needs with operational flexibility.

When implementing emergency stop patterns, careful consideration must be given to the scope of what can be paused. Rather than implementing a single global pause mechanism, contracts often benefit from granular pause controls that can target specific functions or components. This approach allows for more precise risk management while maintaining essential functionality during incidents.

Access control for emergency stop mechanisms is crucial. The ability to pause and unpause contract functionality should be strictly limited to authorized addresses, typically through a robust role-based access control system. Many implementations use a tiered approach where different roles have different pause capabilities, allowing for rapid response from operational teams while maintaining appropriate governance controls.

One common pattern is to implement multiple pause levels that correspond to different severity levels of emergencies. For example, a contract might have a "soft pause" that temporarily suspends new transactions while allowing existing positions to be closed, and a "hard pause" that freezes all functionality except basic withdrawals. This granular control allows for proportional responses to different types of emergencies.

Recovery mechanisms are an essential companion to emergency stops. Contracts should implement clear procedures for resuming normal operations once the emergency has been resolved. This includes consideration of state transitions, accumulated values, and any temporary data that needs to be reconciled when the contract is unpaused.

Time-based considerations play an important role in emergency stop patterns. Implementing cooldown periods between pause and unpause actions can prevent rapid toggling of contract states that might be exploited by attackers. Additionally, automatic timeout mechanisms can ensure that paused contracts don't remain indefinitely frozen without explicit governance action.

Event emission is crucial for emergency stop functionality. Every pause and unpause action should emit detailed events that include the caller's address, timestamp, and any relevant context about the emergency. These events are essential for monitoring, auditing, and coordinating responses to security incidents.

Storage considerations become important when implementing emergency stops in complex systems. The pause state should be efficiently stored and accessed, particularly in proxy-based upgradeable contracts where storage layout must be carefully managed. Consider using dedicated storage contracts for pause state in complex systems with multiple components.

Gas optimization remains important even in emergency scenarios. While emergency functions might be called infrequently, they should still be implemented efficiently to ensure they remain executable under high network load or gas price spikes. This is particularly important for unpause functions that might need to be called during network stress events.

Integration with external protocols requires careful handling of emergency stops. Contracts that interact with other protocols should implement pause mechanisms that safely handle external state changes and maintain consistency across protocol boundaries. Consider implementing fallback mechanisms for critical external interactions that might be affected by paused functionality.

Testing emergency stop functionality requires comprehensive scenarios that cover various pause states and transition paths. Tests should verify that paused contracts properly restrict access to protected functions while maintaining critical operations like withdrawals. Include tests for edge cases around pause state transitions and permission boundaries.

Monitoring systems should be configured to provide immediate alerts when emergency stop functions are triggered. Implement detailed logging and analytics around pause states to help teams quickly diagnose and respond to emergencies. Consider implementing automated circuit breakers that can trigger pause mechanisms based on predefined risk parameters.

Documentation for emergency stop mechanisms should be extremely clear and accessible. Operations teams need to understand exactly how to trigger emergency stops and what the implications are for different pause states. Include detailed runbooks for emergency scenarios and clear procedures for coordinating responses across team members.

User interface considerations are important for emergency stops. Applications should clearly communicate pause states to users and provide appropriate guidance about restricted functionality. Implement clear error messages that help users understand why certain operations are unavailable during pause states.

Governance mechanisms often need to interact with emergency stops. Implement appropriate voting or multi-signature requirements for permanent changes to pause mechanisms while maintaining the ability for rapid response to emergencies. Consider implementing tiered governance where emergency actions can be taken quickly but require subsequent ratification.

Upgradeability patterns must carefully consider emergency stop functionality. Ensure that pause mechanisms remain functional across contract upgrades and that pause states are properly preserved. Implement version tracking for pause mechanisms to maintain compatibility with existing monitoring and governance systems.

The future of emergency stop patterns continues to evolve with new security challenges and protocol designs. Stay informed about emerging best practices and consider implementing advanced features like automated circuit breakers and cross-chain emergency coordination. Regular review and updates of emergency procedures help maintain effective security responses in an evolving ecosystem.

26. Secure Multi-Signature Wallets

Secure multi-signature wallets represent one of the most critical security patterns in smart contract development, providing a robust mechanism for managing high-value assets and sensitive operations through distributed control. These contracts require multiple parties to approve transactions before execution, significantly reducing the risk of unauthorized access and single points of failure.

The fundamental architecture of a secure multi-signature wallet begins with careful consideration of the signing mechanism. Rather than relying on a single private key, multi-signature wallets implement a system where a threshold of approved signers must consent to any transaction. This threshold is typically defined during contract deployment and might require, for example, two out of three or three out of five signatures for transaction execution.

Implementation of multi-signature functionality requires careful handling of cryptographic signatures. The contract must verify that signatures are valid, properly formatted, and come from authorized signers. This verification process typically involves ecrecover to extract signer addresses from signatures, along with careful checks to prevent signature replay attacks and ensure signature uniqueness.

Transaction proposal and execution in multi-signature wallets follows a two-step process. First, a transaction is proposed, creating a unique identifier and storing the transaction details. Second, other authorized signers can submit their approvals until the required threshold is met. Once sufficient signatures are collected, the transaction can be executed. This separation of proposal and execution provides important safety guarantees and allows for careful review of proposed transactions.

Storage considerations become particularly important in multi-signature implementations. The contract must efficiently track pending transactions, signature status, and signer authorities while minimizing gas costs. Many implementations use mapping structures to track transaction states and signatures, with careful consideration given to cleanup of executed or expired transactions to prevent state bloat.

Nonce management plays a crucial role in preventing transaction replay attacks. Each transaction proposal should include a unique nonce that increments with each execution, ensuring that signatures cannot be reused for multiple transactions. Some implementations use per-signer nonces for additional security, though this increases complexity and gas costs.

Time-based constraints often form an important part of multi-signature security. Implementing expiration times for pending transactions prevents old proposals from being executed under changed circumstances. Similarly, time locks can be implemented for certain high-value operations, providing additional security through mandatory delay periods.

Error handling in multi-signature wallets must be particularly robust. Failed transactions should preserve the contract's state and provide clear error messages. Consider implementing recovery mechanisms for scenarios where signers become unavailable or keys are compromised. Some implementations include procedures for signer replacement or threshold adjustment through existing multi-signature consensus.

Gas optimization becomes crucial when multiple signatures are required. Batch signature verification can reduce gas costs compared to individual verification. Consider implementing signature aggregation techniques where appropriate, though carefully weigh the complexity tradeoffs. Some implementations allow for gas payment by any party to increase flexibility in transaction execution.

Event emission should be comprehensive in multi-signature contracts. Every significant action such as transaction proposal, signature submission, and execution should emit detailed events. These events are crucial for off-chain monitoring and coordination between signers, as well as providing a clear audit trail of wallet activities.

Integration with external contracts requires careful consideration in multi-signature contexts. When the wallet interacts with other contracts, ensure that the interaction patterns are compatible with the multi-signature approval process. Consider implementing specialized handling for common interaction patterns like token transfers or protocol governance actions.

Testing multi-signature implementations requires comprehensive scenarios covering various signer combinations and edge cases. Include tests for signature validation, threshold checking, nonce management, and transaction execution. Pay particular attention to testing recovery mechanisms and governance operations that modify wallet parameters.

User interface considerations are particularly important for multi-signature wallets. Signers need clear information about pending transactions, signature status, and execution requirements. Implement clear messaging around transaction proposals and signature requirements to prevent confusion and errors in the signing process.

Security analysis of multi-signature implementations should consider various attack vectors. Protect against signature malleability, replay attacks, and front-running. Implement proper access controls for administrative functions and consider the implications of contract upgrades on signature validity.

Recovery mechanisms deserve special attention in multi-signature designs. Consider scenarios like lost keys, compromised signers, or technical failures. Implement appropriate procedures for signer replacement and threshold adjustment while maintaining security guarantees. Some implementations include delayed recovery procedures that provide time for monitoring and intervention.

Documentation for multi-signature wallets should be extremely detailed, covering both technical implementation details and operational procedures. Include clear instructions for signature creation, transaction proposal, and execution. Document recovery procedures and governance mechanisms thoroughly to ensure operational teams can respond effectively to various scenarios.

Upgradeability in multi-signature contracts requires careful handling of signature verification and state management. Ensure that upgrade procedures maintain signature validity and don't introduce vulnerabilities in the verification process. Consider implementing version tracking for signature schemes to maintain compatibility across upgrades.

The evolution of multi-signature patterns continues with new developments in cryptography and blockchain technology. Consider implementing emerging standards for signature schemes and exploring advanced features like threshold signature schemes or multi-party computation. Regular review of implementation patterns helps maintain security as the ecosystem evolves.

27. Batch Operation Security

Batch operations in smart contracts provide significant efficiency gains by allowing multiple transactions or state changes to be processed in a single blockchain transaction. However, this efficiency comes with unique security considerations that must be carefully addressed to prevent vulnerabilities and ensure consistent contract state.

The primary motivation for implementing batch operations is gas optimization. By combining multiple operations into a single transaction, we can amortize fixed gas costs and reduce the overall cost of contract interactions. This is particularly valuable in scenarios involving token transfers, NFT minting, or complex state updates that would otherwise require multiple separate transactions.

When implementing batch operations, array handling becomes a critical security concern. Smart contracts must carefully validate array lengths and ensure consistency between multiple input arrays. A common vulnerability arises when different input arrays have mismatched lengths, potentially leading to partial execution or unexpected state changes. Implement strict length validation before processing any batch operations.

Gas limits present another significant consideration in batch operation design. Each operation in a batch consumes gas, and the total gas consumption must remain within block gas limits. Implement mechanisms to estimate gas consumption and limit batch sizes appropriately. Consider providing functions that allow users to estimate gas requirements before submitting transactions.

State consistency must be maintained throughout batch processing. If any operation in the batch fails, the contract must handle the failure appropriately. Consider implementing atomic execution patterns where either all operations succeed or the entire batch reverts.

This prevents partial state changes that could leave the contract in an inconsistent state.

Reentrancy protection becomes more complex with batch operations. When processing multiple external calls within a batch, ensure that proper reentrancy guards are in place. Consider implementing a single reentrancy guard for the entire batch operation rather than individual guards for each call to optimize gas usage while maintaining security.

Input validation in batch operations must be thorough and efficient. Validate all inputs before beginning any state changes to prevent partial execution with invalid data. Consider implementing validation helper functions that can be reused across different batch operations. Balance validation thoroughness with gas efficiency to maintain practical usability.

Error handling strategies for batch operations should provide clear feedback about failures. Consider implementing detailed error reporting that identifies which operations in a batch failed and why. This information helps users and integrating systems understand and resolve issues effectively. Some implementations return success/failure arrays indicating the status of each operation.

Access control for batch operations requires careful consideration. Determine whether all operations in a batch should require the same permissions or if different operations can have different access requirements. Implement efficient permission checking that doesn't unnecessarily duplicate checks across batch items while maintaining security.

Event emission in batch operations should provide sufficient detail for monitoring and auditing. Consider whether to emit events for each individual operation or aggregate events for the entire batch. Balance the tradeoff between gas efficiency and granularity of event data based on specific use case requirements.

Memory management becomes particularly important in batch operations. Large arrays and complex data structures can consume significant memory. Implement efficient memory usage patterns and consider breaking extremely large batches into smaller chunks to prevent out-of-gas errors and excessive memory consumption.

Integration with other contracts in batch operations requires careful design. When interacting with multiple external contracts, consider the implications of failed calls and how they affect the overall batch operation. Implement appropriate error handling and state management for external interactions.

Testing batch operations requires comprehensive scenarios covering various input combinations and edge cases. Test with different batch sizes, including empty batches, single-item batches, and maximum-size batches. Include tests for partial failures, invalid inputs, and gas limit scenarios.

Gas optimization in batch operations extends beyond simple operation combining. Consider implementing sorted operations to minimize storage updates, batched storage reads and writes, and efficient data encoding patterns. Balance these optimizations against code complexity and maintainability.

Documentation for batch operations should clearly specify size limits, gas considerations, and error handling behavior. Include examples of proper batch construction and handling of operation results. Document any requirements for input ordering or formatting that affect operation success.

Monitoring batch operations in production requires attention to transaction success rates and gas usage patterns. Implement appropriate logging and alerting for batch failures or unusual patterns. Consider providing tools or interfaces that help users construct efficient batches.

Upgradeability considerations for batch operations include maintaining compatibility with existing batch formats and ensuring that state changes remain consistent across upgrades. Consider versioning batch operation interfaces to allow for future improvements while maintaining backward compatibility.

Front-running protection may be necessary for certain types of batch operations. Consider implementing commit-reveal schemes or other mechanisms to prevent manipulation of batch execution order. Balance these protections against their impact on usability and gas costs.

Recovery mechanisms for failed batch operations should be clearly defined. Consider implementing retry mechanisms for failed operations or providing ways to extract and resubmit failed items from a batch. Ensure that recovery mechanisms maintain proper access controls and state consistency.

The evolution of batch operation patterns continues with new optimization techniques and security considerations. Regular review of implementation patterns and emerging standards helps maintain efficient and secure batch processing capabilities as the ecosystem develops.

28. State Machine Patterns

State machine patterns represent a fundamental approach to modeling complex smart contract behavior in a secure and predictable manner. By explicitly defining contract states and the valid transitions between them, developers can create robust systems that maintain consistency and prevent unauthorized or illogical operations.

A state machine in smart contracts consists of distinct states that represent different conditions or phases of contract operation. Each state has specific rules about which operations are permitted and which transitions can occur. This explicit modeling helps prevent invalid operations and maintains contract integrity throughout its lifecycle.

The foundation of implementing state machine patterns begins with clearly defining the possible states. States should be comprehensive, mutually exclusive, and represent meaningful distinctions in contract behavior. Common implementations use enums or constants to represent states, providing clear and gas efficient state tracking. Each state should be documented with its intended purpose and the conditions under which it applies.

Transition functions form the core of state machine implementation. These functions handle the logic for moving between states and must include appropriate validation to ensure only valid transitions occur. Implement guards and require statements to verify that transitions are authorized and conditions are met before allowing state changes. Consider using modifiers to enforce state dependent behavior across multiple functions.

Access control in state machines must be carefully integrated with state transitions. Different roles may have different permissions to initiate state transitions. Implement role based access control that considers both the current state and the requested transition. Some transitions may require multiple approvals or specific conditions to be met before proceeding.

Event emission plays a crucial role in state machine transparency. Emit events for all state transitions to provide an auditable trail of contract progression. Include relevant details such as the previous state, new state, initiator of the transition, and any pertinent conditions or parameters that influenced the transition. This event trail helps with monitoring and debugging contract behavior.

Error handling in state machines should provide clear feedback about why transitions fail. Implement custom error messages that specifically identify whether failures occur due to invalid state transitions, insufficient permissions, or unmet conditions. This specificity helps users and integrating systems understand and correct issues effectively.

Timeouts and automatic transitions require careful consideration in state machine design. Some states may have maximum durations or conditions that trigger automatic transitions. Implement these automatic transitions securely, considering the implications of block timestamps and potential manipulation. Include appropriate checks and balances to prevent gaming of timeout mechanisms.

Reentrance protection becomes particularly important in state machines with external calls. State transitions should complete fully before allowing new operations. Implement reentrancy guards that protect not only individual functions but ensure the integrity of state progression. Consider the implications of nested state machines when integrating with other contracts.

Testing state machines requires comprehensive coverage of all possible transitions and edge cases. Implement tests that verify both valid and invalid transition attempts from each state. Include tests for permission requirements, condition checking, and automatic transitions. Test timeout mechanisms and ensure proper event emission for all state changes.

Gas optimization in state machine implementation requires balancing clarity with efficiency. Consider using bit mapping for complex state tracking where appropriate. Optimize storage usage by combining related state data into packed structures. Balance these optimizations against code readability and maintenance requirements.

Documentation for state machines should include clear state diagrams showing all possible transitions. Document the conditions required for each transition, the roles that can initiate them, and any time based or external conditions that affect state progression. Include examples of typical state progression patterns for common use cases.

Recovery mechanisms in state machines should account for edge cases and exceptional conditions. Implement emergency functions that allow authorized roles to resolve stuck states or correct invalid conditions. These recovery mechanisms must maintain proper access controls and emit appropriate events to maintain transparency.

State machine composition becomes important in complex systems. Multiple state machines may need to interact or coordinate their states. Implement clear interfaces between state machines and consider the implications of state dependencies. Document the relationships between different state machines in the system.

Upgradeability considerations for state machines include maintaining state consistency across upgrades. Consider how state definitions and transition rules might need to evolve over time. Implement upgrade mechanisms that can properly migrate existing states and preserve the integrity of state progression history.

Monitoring state machines in production requires attention to transition patterns and timing. Implement appropriate logging and alerting for unexpected state conditions or transition failures. Consider providing interfaces that help users understand current state and available transitions.

The evolution of state machine patterns continues with new implementation techniques and security considerations. Regular review of implementation patterns and emerging standards helps maintain robust and secure state management as contract complexity increases. Consider incorporating formal verification techniques to prove the correctness of state transition logic.

State machines provide a powerful pattern for managing complex contract behavior, but their effectiveness depends on careful implementation and thorough testing. By following these principles and considerations, developers can create reliable and secure state based systems that maintain consistency throughout their operation.

29. Oracle Integration Security

Oracle integration security represents a critical aspect of smart contract development, as oracles serve as the bridge between blockchain networks and external data sources. Understanding how to securely implement and interact with oracles is essential for creating reliable decentralized applications that depend on real world information.

The fundamental challenge in oracle integration lies in maintaining the trustless nature of blockchain systems while incorporating external data. Oracles introduce potential points of failure and security vulnerabilities that must be carefully managed. Implementing proper validation, redundancy, and failure handling mechanisms becomes crucial for maintaining contract security.

Data source verification forms the first line of defense in oracle security. Implement thorough validation of data sources, including authenticity checks and signature verification where applicable. Consider using multiple independent data sources and implementing consensus mechanisms to prevent manipulation by single sources. Document the trust assumptions and verification methods for each data source.

Rate limiting and update frequency must be carefully controlled in oracle implementations. Excessive updates can lead to increased gas costs and potential attack vectors. Implement appropriate cooldown periods between updates and consider the implications of update frequency on contract security. Balance the need for timely data with the security implications of update mechanisms.

Data validation in oracle implementations must account for both format and reasonableness. Implement range checks and format validation for incoming data. Consider implementing circuit breakers that trigger when data falls outside expected parameters. Include mechanisms to handle temporary data unavailability without compromising contract security.

Redundancy in oracle systems provides protection against individual oracle failures or manipulation. Implement aggregation mechanisms that combine data from multiple sources. Consider weighted averaging or median selection algorithms that can handle outliers and attempted manipulation. Document the redundancy mechanisms and their failure modes.

Access control for oracle updates requires careful consideration. Implement proper permissions for oracle update functions and consider using time locks or multi signature requirements for sensitive updates. Include mechanisms to revoke compromised oracle access and migrate to new data sources when necessary.

Gas considerations become particularly important in oracle implementations. Optimize update mechanisms to minimize gas costs while maintaining security. Consider implementing batching mechanisms for multiple updates when appropriate. Balance the frequency of updates against the gas costs of storage and computation.

Error handling in oracle integration must account for various failure modes. Implement fallback mechanisms for when oracle data is unavailable or invalid. Consider the implications of delayed or failed updates on contract operation. Include appropriate event emission to track oracle related issues.

Version management for oracle interfaces requires careful planning. Implement upgrade paths that can accommodate changes in data sources or oracle protocols. Consider backwards compatibility requirements and data format evolution. Document version dependencies and upgrade procedures.

Testing oracle integrations requires comprehensive simulation of various failure modes. Implement tests that verify behavior under normal conditions and various error scenarios. Include tests for data validation, access control, and redundancy mechanisms. Consider fuzzing tests to identify edge cases in data handling.

Monitoring oracle operation becomes crucial for maintaining security. Implement logging and alerting for unusual patterns or potential manipulation attempts. Consider implementing dashboards or monitoring interfaces that track oracle performance and data quality. Document monitoring requirements and response procedures.

Economic security in oracle systems must consider potential attack vectors and incentives. Implement appropriate bonds or stake requirements for oracle operators where applicable. Consider the economic implications of oracle manipulation and implement appropriate safeguards. Document the economic security model and its assumptions.

Cross chain oracle considerations become important in multi chain environments. Implement appropriate verification for cross chain oracle data. Consider the implications of different chain finality and block times. Document cross chain dependencies and security assumptions.

Privacy considerations in oracle implementations must balance transparency with data sensitivity. Implement appropriate encryption or data masking where required. Consider the implications of public blockchain data availability on oracle security. Document privacy requirements and implementation methods.

Recovery mechanisms for oracle failures should be clearly defined. Implement procedures for handling extended oracle downtime or compromise. Consider fallback data sources and recovery procedures. Document incident response procedures for various oracle failure scenarios.

Oracle upgrade patterns should maintain security throughout the upgrade process. Implement mechanisms to verify new oracle implementations before activation. Consider gradual migration strategies that maintain system stability. Document upgrade procedures and verification requirements.

Integration with existing oracle networks requires careful consideration of security implications. Implement appropriate interfaces and validation for network specific requirements. Consider the security track record and reliability of oracle networks. Document integration requirements and security assumptions.

The future of oracle security continues to evolve with new protocols and security patterns. Stay informed about emerging oracle security standards and best practices. Consider implementing new security features as they become available. Maintain documentation of security improvements and evolving requirements.

Oracle integration security requires ongoing attention to maintain the integrity of smart contract systems. Regular security reviews and updates help ensure that oracle implementations remain robust against emerging threats. By following these principles and considerations, developers can create secure and reliable oracle integrations that maintain the trustless properties of blockchain systems while incorporating essential external data.

30. Cross-Contract Communication

Cross contract communication represents a fundamental aspect of modern smart contract development, enabling complex interactions between different contracts on the blockchain. Understanding how to implement secure communication patterns between contracts is essential for building robust decentralized applications that maintain security across contract boundaries.

The foundation of cross contract communication lies in understanding the different methods contracts can interact with each other. Direct function calls, delegate calls, and message passing each present unique security considerations that must be carefully managed. The choice of communication method significantly impacts the security model and potential vulnerabilities of the system.

Contract interfaces form the basis for secure cross contract communication. Properly defined interfaces ensure type safety and function signature compatibility between contracts. Interface definitions should be carefully versioned and documented to maintain compatibility across contract updates. Consider implementing interface detection mechanisms to verify contract compatibility at runtime.

Address validation becomes crucial when implementing cross contract communication. Always verify that target contract addresses are valid and implement checks to prevent calls to unintended contracts. Consider implementing address registries or whitelisting mechanisms for approved contract interactions. Include mechanisms to update contract references securely when needed.

Return value handling requires careful attention in cross contract calls. Never assume that external calls will succeed and always check return values. Implement appropriate error handling for failed calls and consider the implications of partial execution. Document expected return values and error conditions for all cross contract interactions.

Reentrancy protection becomes particularly important when implementing cross contract communication. Implement checks effects interactions pattern consistently across contract boundaries. Consider the implications of nested calls and potential reentrant paths through multiple contracts. Document reentrancy assumptions and protection mechanisms.

State consistency across contracts must be carefully maintained. Implement appropriate locking or synchronization mechanisms when necessary. Consider the implications of failed calls on cross contract state consistency. Include mechanisms to recover from partially completed cross contract operations.

Gas forwarding and management requires careful consideration in cross contract calls. Understand how gas is consumed across contract boundaries and implement appropriate gas limits. Consider the implications of out of gas conditions on cross contract operations. Document gas requirements and limitations for contract interactions.

Error propagation across contract boundaries needs proper handling. Implement consistent error handling patterns that maintain security across contract boundaries. Consider how errors in one contract affect dependent contracts. Document error handling expectations and recovery procedures.

Version compatibility between contracts requires careful management. Implement appropriate version checking mechanisms for cross contract calls. Consider the implications of contract upgrades on cross contract compatibility. Document version dependencies and upgrade procedures.

Access control across contract boundaries must be consistently enforced. Implement appropriate permission checks for cross contract calls. Consider the security implications of delegated calls and permission inheritance. Document access control requirements and verification procedures.

Event emission for cross contract operations provides important audit trails. Implement consistent event logging patterns across contract boundaries. Consider the implications of cross contract events on system monitoring. Document event requirements and monitoring procedures.

Testing cross contract interactions requires comprehensive scenarios. Implement tests that verify behavior across contract boundaries under various conditions. Include tests for error conditions and partial execution scenarios. Consider integration tests that verify complete cross contract workflows.

Security considerations for delegate calls require special attention. Understand the security implications of execution context in delegate calls. Implement appropriate access controls and validation for delegate call targets. Document delegate call usage and security assumptions.

Upgrade patterns for cross contract systems must maintain security. Implement upgrade mechanisms that preserve cross contract compatibility. Consider the implications of partial upgrades on system security. Document upgrade procedures and verification requirements.

State isolation between contracts should be carefully maintained. Implement appropriate encapsulation of contract state. Consider the implications of shared state and storage patterns. Document state management requirements and isolation mechanisms.

Economic security across contract boundaries requires careful consideration. Implement appropriate value transfer controls between contracts. Consider the implications of economic attacks across contract boundaries. Document economic security assumptions and protections.

Cross chain considerations become important in multi chain environments. Implement appropriate verification for cross chain contract interactions. Consider the implications of different chain characteristics on security. Document cross chain dependencies and security requirements.

Privacy implications of cross contract calls must be considered. Understand how contract interactions affect data visibility. Implement appropriate data protection mechanisms across contract boundaries. Document privacy requirements and implementation approaches.

Recovery mechanisms for failed cross contract operations should be defined. Implement appropriate rollback or compensation mechanisms. Consider the implications of partial failure on system state. Document recovery procedures for various failure scenarios.

Monitoring cross contract interactions becomes crucial for security. Implement appropriate logging and alerting for unusual patterns. Consider implementing dashboards or monitoring interfaces that track cross contract operations. Document monitoring requirements and response procedures.

The future of cross contract communication continues to evolve with new patterns and protocols. Stay informed about emerging standards and security best practices. Consider implementing new security features as they become available. Maintain documentation of security improvements and evolving requirements.

Cross contract communication security requires ongoing attention to maintain system integrity. Regular security reviews and updates help ensure that contract interactions remain secure and reliable. By following these principles and considerations, developers can create robust cross contract systems that maintain security across contract boundaries while enabling complex decentralized applications.

31. Testing Framework Setup

Testing Framework Setup forms the foundation of a robust smart contract development process. A well-configured testing environment enables developers to catch bugs early, validate functionality, and ensure security throughout the development lifecycle. This chapter explores the essential components and best practices for establishing a comprehensive testing framework for Solidity smart contracts.

The primary testing framework for Ethereum smart contract development is Hardhat, though alternatives like Truffle and Foundry also offer powerful testing capabilities. Setting up a testing framework begins with initializing a new project and installing the necessary dependencies. This includes the testing framework itself, assertion libraries, and helpful utilities for contract deployment and interaction.

Configuration of the testing environment requires careful consideration of network settings. Local development networks, testnets, and mainnet forks each serve different testing purposes. Local networks provide rapid feedback during development, while testnet deployments validate behavior in more realistic conditions. Mainnet forks enable testing against production state and contract interactions.

Test file organization plays a crucial role in maintaining a manageable test suite. Structure test files to mirror the organization of your smart contracts, with separate test files for each contract. Group related tests into describe blocks that clearly indicate the functionality being tested. Include setup and teardown procedures to ensure a clean testing environment for each test case.

Environment variables management becomes essential for secure testing. Never commit sensitive information like private keys or API endpoints directly in test files. Instead, utilize environment configuration files and load sensitive data dynamically. Implement proper gitignore patterns to prevent accidental exposure of sensitive information.

Contract deployment scripts form an integral part of the testing framework. Create reusable deployment scripts that handle contract initialization and configuration. Include mechanisms to verify deployed contract addresses and state. Consider implementing deployment fixtures that can be shared across multiple test files.

Test helpers and utilities significantly improve testing efficiency. Develop helper functions for common operations like time manipulation, mining blocks, and contract interaction. Create utilities for converting between different number formats and handling complex data structures. Document helper functions thoroughly to enable team-wide usage.

Mocking capabilities become crucial for isolating components during testing. Implement contract mocks that simulate external dependencies and complex interactions. Create utilities for generating test data and simulating various network conditions. Consider implementing mock factories for generating test scenarios.

Gas reporting provides important optimization insights during testing. Configure gas reporters to track gas usage across different function calls. Implement gas benchmarking for critical operations. Consider setting gas limits for tests to catch unexpected gas consumption patterns.

Test coverage analysis helps identify untested code paths. Configure coverage tools to track which contract code is exercised by tests. Set coverage thresholds as part of the continuous integration process. Regular review coverage reports to identify areas needing additional testing.

Console output formatting improves test result readability. Configure test runners to provide clear, structured output of test results. Implement custom reporters for specific testing needs. Consider color coding output to highlight important information.

Snapshot testing capabilities enable verification of complex contract states. Implement mechanisms to capture and verify contract state snapshots. Create utilities for comparing states before and after operations. Consider implementing differential testing approaches for complex state changes.

Performance testing requires specific framework configuration. Implement benchmarking capabilities for measuring execution time and gas usage. Create stress testing scenarios for high load conditions. Consider implementing performance regression testing as part of the continuous integration pipeline.

Debug capabilities significantly improve the testing experience. Configure debugger integration for stepping through contract execution. Implement logging utilities for tracking contract behavior. Consider implementing debug modes for additional visibility during testing.

Test data management requires careful consideration. Implement fixtures for generating consistent test data. Create utilities for managing complex test scenarios. Consider implementing data factories for generating varied test cases.

Continuous integration setup ensures consistent test execution. Configure automated test runs on code changes. Implement test result reporting and notification systems. Consider implementing parallel test execution for larger test suites.

Network management utilities facilitate testing across different environments. Implement utilities for managing network connections and configurations. Create helpers for handling network specific requirements. Consider implementing network simulation capabilities for edge cases.

Time manipulation capabilities enable testing of time dependent functionality. Implement utilities for advancing blockchain time and manipulating timestamps. Create helpers for testing scheduling and timing related features. Consider implementing time travel capabilities for complex scenarios.

Error injection capabilities enable thorough testing of error handling. Implement utilities for simulating various error conditions. Create helpers for testing recovery mechanisms. Consider implementing chaos testing approaches for robustness verification.

Documentation of the testing framework ensures team wide understanding. Document framework setup and configuration requirements. Create guidelines for writing and organizing tests. Consider implementing automated documentation generation for test utilities.

The testing framework should evolve with project needs. Regularly review and update testing capabilities as requirements change. Implement new testing features as needed. Consider conducting periodic framework audits to ensure effectiveness.

Testing framework maintenance requires ongoing attention. Regular updates of dependencies and security patches. Periodic review of testing patterns and approaches. Consider implementing automated framework maintenance procedures.

By establishing a comprehensive testing framework with these components and considerations, development teams can ensure thorough testing of smart contracts throughout the development lifecycle. Regular framework updates and maintenance ensure continued effectiveness as project requirements evolve.

32. Unit Testing Strategies

Unit Testing Strategies represent a critical component of smart contract development security. Effective unit testing helps identify bugs, validate functionality, and ensure contract behavior meets specifications. This chapter explores comprehensive approaches to unit testing Solidity smart contracts, providing developers with practical strategies for building robust test suites.

Unit tests for smart contracts should follow the Arrange-Act-Assert pattern, which provides a clear structure for test cases. The arrangement phase sets up the test environment, including contract deployment and initial state configuration. The action phase executes the functionality being tested, while the assertion phase verifies the expected outcomes. This pattern helps maintain clarity and consistency across test cases.

Test isolation represents a fundamental principle of unit testing. Each test should run independently of others, with no shared state or dependencies between tests. Implement beforeEach hooks to deploy fresh contract instances for each test case. Use afterEach hooks to clean up any residual state that might affect subsequent tests. This isolation ensures test reliability and makes debugging easier when failures occur.

Testing state transitions requires particular attention in smart contract development. Create test cases that verify contract state before and after operations. Implement checks for both successful state changes and failed attempts. Consider edge cases where state transitions might interact in unexpected ways. Testing state machines thoroughly helps prevent logical errors that could compromise contract security.

Function input validation testing ensures contracts handle various input scenarios correctly. Test both valid and invalid input combinations. Verify error messages and revert conditions for invalid inputs. Include tests for boundary conditions and edge cases. Pay special attention to numerical inputs that might cause overflow or underflow conditions.

Access control testing validates permission systems and role based restrictions. Create test cases for each permission level and role combination. Verify both successful and failed access attempts. Test permission transfers and role assignments. Include scenarios where permissions might interact or conflict. This comprehensive approach helps prevent unauthorized access to critical functions.

Event emission testing verifies correct event logging behavior. Test that events are emitted with correct parameters under appropriate conditions. Verify event ordering when multiple events should be emitted. Include negative tests to ensure events are not emitted inappropriately. Proper event testing helps maintain contract transparency and facilitates external monitoring.

Gas optimization testing measures function execution costs. Implement tests that track gas usage for different operations. Compare gas costs across different implementation approaches. Set maximum gas thresholds for critical functions. Regular gas testing helps identify optimization opportunities and prevent deployment of inefficient code.

Error handling testing ensures contracts manage exceptional conditions appropriately. Test all error conditions and revert scenarios. Verify error messages provide useful information. Include tests for custom error types and error inheritance. Comprehensive error testing helps maintain contract reliability under adverse conditions.

Testing mathematical operations requires special attention to precision and rounding. Implement tests for various numerical scenarios including edge cases. Verify correct handling of decimals and percentage calculations. Test mathematical operations with different order of operations. Include tests for potential precision loss scenarios.

Modifier testing validates the behavior of function modifiers. Create tests for each modifier combination. Verify modifier ordering effects. Test modifier interactions with inheritance. Include tests for modifier revert conditions. Thorough modifier testing helps prevent unexpected function behavior.

Time based logic testing verifies temporal dependencies and scheduling. Implement tests using time manipulation utilities. Verify behavior across different time periods and transitions. Test scheduling and deadline mechanisms. Include tests for time based state changes and restrictions.

Integration point testing validates contract interactions with external dependencies. Create mock contracts to simulate external interactions. Test different response scenarios from external calls. Verify handling of failed external calls. Include tests for callback functions and recursive interactions.

Inheritance testing ensures correct behavior across contract hierarchies. Test function overriding and super calls. Verify state variable shadowing behavior. Test constructor chaining and initialization. Include tests for multiple inheritance scenarios and potential conflicts.

Upgrade testing validates contract upgradeability mechanisms. Test storage layout compatibility. Verify initialization of new versions. Test migration of existing state. Include tests for upgrade access controls and authorization. Comprehensive upgrade testing helps prevent issues during contract evolution.

Testing helper functions requires attention to utility code reliability. Create dedicated test suites for helper functions. Verify helper function edge cases and error conditions. Test helper function performance and gas usage. Include tests for helper function interactions and dependencies.

View and pure function testing validates read only operations. Test view function return values and calculations. Verify pure function deterministic behavior. Include tests for view function gas usage. Test view function access restrictions and permissions.

Batch operation testing ensures correct handling of multiple transactions. Test various batch sizes and composition. Verify partial success scenarios and rollback behavior. Test batch operation gas limitations. Include tests for batch operation ordering effects.

Proxy pattern testing validates delegation and forwarding behavior. Test delegate call functionality and return handling. Verify storage access patterns through proxies. Test upgrade mechanisms and initialization. Include tests for proxy interaction with other contracts.

Documentation testing ensures test coverage aligns with specifications. Verify test cases cover all documented functionality. Test compliance with technical specifications. Include tests for documented limitations and restrictions. Regular documentation testing helps maintain alignment between code and specifications.

Unit testing strategies should evolve with project requirements and complexity. Regular review and updates of test suites ensure continued effectiveness. Consider implementing automated test generation for common patterns. Maintain clear documentation of testing approaches and rationale.

By implementing these comprehensive unit testing strategies, developers can build robust test suites that validate contract functionality and security. Regular review and enhancement of testing approaches ensures continued effectiveness as contracts evolve and requirements change.

33. Integration Testing Approaches

Integration testing for smart contracts represents a crucial layer of validation that ensures different components work together correctly in a real-world environment. While unit tests focus on isolated components, integration tests verify the interactions between multiple contracts, external systems, and various network conditions. This chapter explores comprehensive approaches to integration testing for secure smart contract systems.

Integration testing begins with establishing a testing environment that closely mirrors production conditions. This includes deploying multiple interconnected contracts, setting up test networks with realistic parameters, and simulating various network states. Unlike unit tests, integration tests often require more complex setup procedures and may involve multiple transaction sequences to establish the desired testing state.

Testing contract interactions forms the cornerstone of integration testing. This involves validating how contracts communicate with each other, handle data passing, and manage shared state. Developers should create test scenarios that cover both successful interactions and failure cases, including scenarios where contracts might be upgraded or replaced. Pay particular attention to testing callback patterns, recursive calls, and complex multi-contract transactions.

State synchronization testing ensures that multiple contracts maintain consistent state across interactions. This includes verifying that state changes in one contract properly reflect in dependent contracts, testing state recovery mechanisms, and validating state consistency across different network conditions. Create test cases that simulate network congestion, delayed transactions, and out of order execution to ensure robust state handling.

External dependency integration requires careful testing of oracle interactions, price feeds, and other external data sources. Create test scenarios that simulate various external conditions, including delayed responses, invalid data, and service outages. Implement tests for fallback mechanisms and contingency handling when external services fail or provide unexpected responses.

Token integration testing validates interactions with various token standards and implementations. This includes testing token transfers, approvals, and complex token operations across multiple contracts. Verify proper handling of different token decimals, transfer restrictions, and custom token behaviors. Include tests for token recovery mechanisms and safety checks.

Events and logging integration ensures proper propagation of events across contract interactions. Test that events from different contracts maintain proper ordering and contain accurate information. Verify that monitoring systems can correctly interpret and process events from multiple sources. Include tests for event filtering and aggregation across contract boundaries.

Upgrade coordination testing validates that contract upgrades maintain system integrity. Test upgrade sequences involving multiple dependent contracts. Verify that state migrations and initialization procedures work correctly across the entire system. Include tests for partial upgrades and rollback scenarios when upgrades fail.

Permission and role management integration requires testing access control systems across multiple contracts. Verify that role assignments and permission changes properly propagate through the system. Test delegation mechanisms and permission inheritance across contract boundaries. Include scenarios for permission conflicts and resolution procedures.

Gas optimization testing at the integration level focuses on transaction costs across complex operations. Measure gas consumption for operations involving multiple contracts. Identify potential optimization opportunities in cross contract communications. Set realistic gas limits for complex operations and verify proper handling of out of gas scenarios.

Error propagation testing ensures that errors are handled appropriately across contract boundaries. Verify that error conditions in one contract properly influence dependent contracts. Test error recovery mechanisms and state consistency after failed operations. Include scenarios for custom error types and error handling across different contract versions.

Batch operation integration testing validates the execution of multiple operations across different contracts. Test various batch sizes and composition strategies. Verify proper handling of partial success scenarios and transaction ordering. Include tests for gas limitations and optimal batch sizing under different network conditions.

Time synchronization testing ensures proper handling of temporal dependencies across contracts. Test time based operations involving multiple contracts. Verify proper ordering of time sensitive operations. Include tests for different network timing conditions and block time variations.

Network specific integration testing addresses peculiarities of different blockchain networks. Test contract behavior across different network configurations. Verify gas price strategies and transaction priorities. Include tests for network specific features and limitations.

Load testing at the integration level validates system performance under stress. Simulate high transaction volumes across multiple contracts. Test concurrent operation handling and resource utilization. Verify system stability under various load patterns and network conditions.

Security integration testing focuses on potential vulnerabilities in contract interactions. Test for reentrancy across contract boundaries. Verify access control effectiveness in complex operations. Include tests for front running protection and transaction ordering dependencies.

Monitoring integration ensures proper system observability. Test logging and monitoring systems across multiple contracts. Verify alert mechanisms and threshold monitoring. Include tests for various monitoring scenarios and reporting requirements.

Integration testing should follow a systematic approach with clear documentation of test scenarios and coverage. Maintain comprehensive test suites that evolve with system requirements. Regular review and updates ensure continued effectiveness of integration testing strategies.

By implementing thorough integration testing approaches, developers can ensure their smart contract systems function correctly as complete solutions rather than just individual components. This comprehensive testing strategy helps identify and prevent issues that might only appear in production environments where multiple contracts and systems interact in complex ways.

34. Security Testing Methodologies

Security testing methodologies for smart contracts require a systematic and comprehensive approach to identify vulnerabilities and ensure robust contract security. This chapter explores various methodologies and techniques for conducting thorough security testing of smart contract systems.

Static analysis forms the foundation of security testing, involving systematic examination of contract code without execution. This includes analyzing control flow, data flow, and state transitions to identify potential vulnerabilities. Tools like Slither, Mythril, and Securify can automate this process, but human review remains essential for understanding context and business logic implications.

Fuzzing represents a dynamic testing approach where contracts are subjected to random or semi-random inputs to discover unexpected behaviors. Advanced fuzzing tools like Echidna can generate test cases that explore edge cases and unusual input combinations. This methodology is particularly effective at finding input validation issues, arithmetic errors, and unexpected state transitions.

Symbolic execution testing uses mathematical models to analyze all possible execution paths through a contract. Tools like Manticore can identify paths that lead to vulnerable states or security violations. This methodology excels at finding complex vulnerabilities that might be missed by traditional testing approaches, though it can be computationally intensive for large contracts.

Property based testing involves defining invariants that should hold true throughout contract execution. These properties might include balance consistency, access control invariants, or business logic constraints. Tools like Brownie's hypothesis integration can generate test cases that attempt to violate these properties, helping identify subtle security issues.

Mutation testing evaluates the effectiveness of existing security tests by introducing small changes (mutations) to the contract code and verifying that tests detect these changes. This methodology helps identify gaps in test coverage and areas where security assertions might be insufficient. Common mutations include modifying access controls, changing mathematical operations, and altering state updates.

Taint analysis tracks how untrusted input flows through contract execution. This methodology helps identify places where user supplied data might influence critical operations without proper validation. Security testers should pay particular attention to how tainted data affects access controls, financial calculations, and state modifications.

Time travel testing explores contract behavior across different blockchain states and timestamps. This includes testing time sensitive operations, lock periods, and temporal dependencies. Tools like Ganache allow manipulation of block timestamps to verify proper handling of time based security constraints.

Access control testing methodology focuses on systematically verifying permission systems. This includes testing role assignments, permission inheritance, and access restriction effectiveness. Create test scenarios that attempt to bypass access controls through various attack vectors, including indirect calls and delegate calls.

Race condition testing identifies vulnerabilities related to transaction ordering and state dependencies. This methodology includes testing for front running opportunities, transaction ordering dependencies, and state inconsistencies. Tools like Tenderly can help visualize transaction sequences and identify potential race conditions.

Economic attack testing evaluates contract security from a game theory perspective. This includes analyzing profit opportunities from contract manipulation, testing arbitrage scenarios, and identifying economic vulnerabilities. Create test cases that simulate various market conditions and actor behaviors.

Integration security testing examines vulnerabilities that emerge from contract interactions. This methodology includes testing cross contract calls, callback patterns, and external dependencies. Pay particular attention to reentrancy risks, state consistency, and error propagation across contract boundaries.

Upgrade security testing validates the security of contract upgrade mechanisms. This includes testing access controls for upgrades, state migration security, and upgrade atomicity. Create test scenarios for various upgrade paths and potential failure modes.

Oracle security testing focuses on vulnerabilities related to external data dependencies. This methodology includes testing oracle manipulation scenarios, data validation, and fallback mechanisms. Create test cases for various oracle failure modes and data integrity issues.

Gas security testing examines vulnerabilities related to gas consumption and limitations. This includes testing for denial of service via gas exhaustion, gas griefing attacks, and transaction failure handling. Create test scenarios that explore gas related edge cases and optimization attacks.

Event security testing verifies the integrity and reliability of contract events. This methodology includes testing event manipulation scenarios, event ordering dependencies, and event based security controls. Create test cases that verify proper event emission and handling.

Formal verification methodology applies mathematical proof techniques to verify security properties. While more complex than traditional testing, formal verification can provide stronger security guarantees for critical contract components. Tools like Certora and Act support various formal verification approaches.

Security regression testing ensures that security fixes and improvements don't introduce new vulnerabilities. This methodology includes maintaining a comprehensive suite of security tests and regularly running them against contract modifications. Document security test cases and their coverage of known vulnerability classes.

Penetration testing methodology involves attempting to exploit contracts from an attacker's perspective. This includes crafting specific attack transactions, combining multiple vulnerability classes, and attempting to bypass security controls. Document attempted attacks and their outcomes for future reference.

Security testing should evolve with new vulnerability discoveries and attack patterns. Regular updates to testing methodologies and tools help maintain effectiveness against emerging threats. Maintain documentation of testing procedures, findings, and remediation strategies.

Implementing comprehensive security testing methodologies helps identify and prevent vulnerabilities before deployment. Combine multiple testing approaches for maximum coverage and effectiveness. Regular review and updates ensure testing methodologies remain relevant and effective against evolving security threats.

35. Automated Vulnerability Scanning

Automated vulnerability scanning represents a crucial component in the smart contract security testing pipeline, providing developers and auditors with systematic ways to identify potential security issues early in the development process. This chapter explores the various tools, techniques, and best practices for implementing automated vulnerability scanning in smart contract development.

Automated vulnerability scanners analyze smart contract code to detect known vulnerability patterns, coding anti-patterns, and potential security risks. These tools leverage various analysis techniques, including static analysis, symbolic execution, and pattern matching, to provide comprehensive vulnerability detection capabilities.

Mythril stands as one of the most prominent security analysis tools in the Ethereum ecosystem. It employs symbolic execution and SMT solving to detect a wide range of vulnerabilities, including integer overflow/underflow, reentrancy, and access control issues. Mythril can analyze both deployed contracts and source code, providing detailed reports of potential vulnerabilities along with specific transaction sequences that could trigger them.

Slither, developed by Trail of Bits, offers fast and reliable static analysis capabilities. It excels at detecting common vulnerabilities, optimization opportunities, and code quality issues. Slither's architecture allows for easy extension through custom detectors, enabling teams to implement project specific security rules. The tool provides both a command line interface and a Python API for integration into development workflows.

Securify implements a powerful semantic-based security analysis engine. It translates Solidity code into a semantic model and verifies compliance with security patterns. Securify can detect various vulnerability classes, including reentrancy, unrestricted ether flow, and unhandled exceptions. Its analysis provides both violations and warnings, helping developers prioritize security issues.

SmartCheck focuses on static analysis of Solidity source code, identifying potential security, style, and correctness issues. It provides clear explanations of detected issues along with recommendations for remediation. SmartCheck's analysis covers various aspects including deprecated constructs, gas consumption patterns, and potential security vulnerabilities.

MadMax specializes in detecting gas-focused vulnerabilities that could lead to denial of service conditions. It analyzes contracts for patterns that might result in out-of-gas exceptions, infinite loops, and other gas-related issues. This tool proves particularly valuable for complex contracts where gas optimization is crucial.

Automated scanning tools should be integrated into the continuous integration pipeline, ensuring that every code change undergoes security analysis. This integration can be achieved through GitHub Actions, Jenkins, or other CI/CD platforms. Configure the pipeline to fail builds when critical security issues are detected, forcing developers to address vulnerabilities before merging changes.

Proper configuration of vulnerability scanners is essential for effective results. This includes setting appropriate severity thresholds, configuring false positive filters, and customizing detection rules based on project requirements. Teams should maintain documentation of scanner configurations and regularly review and update them as project needs evolve.

False positives represent a significant challenge in automated vulnerability scanning. Tools may flag legitimate code patterns as potential vulnerabilities, requiring human review to validate findings. Develop processes for reviewing and documenting false positives, and maintain whitelists for approved patterns that trigger false positives.

Scanner results should feed into a vulnerability management system that tracks identified issues, their severity, and remediation status. This system should integrate with project management tools and provide clear visibility into security status across the development team. Regular reviews of vulnerability trends help identify areas requiring additional security focus.

Version management of scanning tools is crucial as new vulnerability patterns and detection capabilities emerge. Maintain a versioned configuration of scanning tools and regularly update them to benefit from improved detection capabilities. Document any changes in detection patterns or configuration requirements across versions.

Custom vulnerability detectors can extend standard scanning capabilities to address project specific security requirements. These might include checks for business logic constraints, custom access control patterns, or project specific invariants. Develop and maintain documentation for custom detectors, including their purpose, detection logic, and maintenance requirements.

Scanning performance becomes crucial as projects grow in complexity. Implement strategies for efficient scanning, including incremental analysis, parallel execution, and selective scanning based on changed components. Monitor scanning times and resource usage to maintain reasonable feedback cycles in the development process.

Result interpretation requires security expertise to understand the implications of detected vulnerabilities. Provide training and documentation to help developers understand scanner outputs and appropriate remediation strategies. Maintain a knowledge base of common findings and their solutions to accelerate the remediation process.

Integration with development environments enhances the effectiveness of vulnerability scanning. IDE plugins can provide real time feedback on potential security issues as developers write code. This immediate feedback helps developers learn secure coding patterns and catch issues before they reach version control.

Regular calibration of scanning tools helps maintain their effectiveness. This includes updating detection rules, adjusting severity thresholds, and fine tuning false positive filters based on project experience. Document calibration decisions and their rationale for future reference.

Automated vulnerability scanning represents one component of a comprehensive security strategy. It should complement, not replace, other security practices including manual code review, security testing, and formal verification. Understand the strengths and limitations of automated scanning tools and use them appropriately within the broader security context.

Compliance requirements might influence vulnerability scanning configurations. Some regulatory frameworks specify required security checks or vulnerability management processes. Document how automated scanning tools support compliance requirements and maintain evidence of security checks for audit purposes.

Emergency response procedures should include roles for automated scanning tools. These tools can help quickly assess the impact of newly discovered vulnerability patterns across the codebase. Maintain procedures for emergency scans and result triage during security incidents.

The future of automated vulnerability scanning points toward increased sophistication in detection capabilities, improved accuracy, and better integration with development workflows. Stay informed about emerging tools and techniques in this space, and be prepared to adapt scanning strategies as new capabilities become available.

36. Formal Verification Basics

Formal verification represents a rigorous mathematical approach to proving the correctness and security properties of smart contracts. Unlike traditional testing methods that can only verify specific scenarios, formal verification aims to mathematically prove that a contract behaves correctly under all possible conditions. This powerful technique has become increasingly important in the development of high-stakes smart contracts where absolute certainty about behavior is required.

At its core, formal verification involves expressing the intended behavior of a smart contract as mathematical specifications and then using automated theorem provers to verify that the implementation satisfies these specifications. This process begins with defining formal specifications that capture both the functional requirements and security properties of the contract. These specifications must be precise and unambiguous, often expressed in formal specification languages like TLA+, Coq, or Why3.

Smart contract specifications typically include invariants, pre-conditions, post-conditions, and temporal properties. Invariants describe conditions that must always hold throughout contract execution, such as conservation of tokens in a financial contract. Pre-conditions specify requirements that must be true before a function executes, while post-conditions define the expected state after execution. Temporal properties describe how contract state should evolve over sequences of operations.

Several formal verification tools have emerged specifically for smart contracts. The K Framework, particularly its KEVM implementation, provides a complete formal semantics of the Ethereum Virtual Machine. This allows developers to verify properties of smart contracts at the bytecode level, ensuring that verification accounts for actual execution behavior. Tools like Certora and Act provide more accessible interfaces for specifying and verifying contract properties while maintaining mathematical rigor.

Writing formal specifications requires a different mindset from traditional programming. Developers must think in terms of mathematical properties rather than procedural steps. For example, instead of describing how a token transfer should happen, formal specifications focus on what properties must hold before and after the transfer. This includes properties like "the sum of all balances remains constant" and "no account can spend more tokens than it owns."

State space exploration represents a crucial aspect of formal verification. Verification tools attempt to explore all possible states and transitions of a contract to prove that specified properties hold universally. This exploration can uncover edge cases that might be missed in traditional testing, such as complex interactions between multiple functions or unexpected state combinations.

The challenge of state space explosion often arises in formal verification. As contracts become more complex, the number of possible states grows exponentially, making complete verification computationally intensive or impractical. Techniques like abstraction, modular verification, and compositional reasoning help manage this complexity by breaking verification into smaller, tractable pieces.

Formal verification can prove various security properties of smart contracts. These include access control invariants (only authorized users can perform certain actions), value conservation (tokens cannot be created or destroyed unexpectedly), and temporal safety properties (certain sequences of operations are impossible). Such proofs provide much stronger guarantees than traditional testing approaches.

Integration of formal verification into the development workflow requires careful consideration. While complete formal verification might be impractical for rapid development cycles, critical components can be verified incrementally. Teams should identify high-risk components that warrant formal verification and develop appropriate specifications for these components early in the development process.

Tool selection for formal verification depends on various factors including the type of properties to be verified, the complexity of the contracts, and the team's expertise. Some tools focus on specific types of properties or provide different tradeoffs between automation and expressiveness. Teams should evaluate available tools based on their specific verification needs and resources.

Documentation plays a crucial role in formal verification. Specifications must be clearly documented, explaining both the mathematical properties being verified and their relationship to business requirements. This documentation helps maintain verification efforts over time and assists in reviewing and updating specifications as requirements evolve.

Training represents a significant investment when adopting formal verification. Teams need to develop expertise in formal methods, specification languages, and verification tools. This includes understanding mathematical concepts like predicate logic, temporal logic, and invariant reasoning. Regular training sessions and knowledge sharing help build and maintain this expertise.

Modular verification strategies help manage complexity in larger systems. By verifying components independently and then composing these verifications, teams can tackle complex systems that would be intractable to verify as a whole. This requires careful attention to interface specifications and composition rules.

Formal verification complements rather than replaces other security practices. While it provides strong guarantees about specified properties, it cannot verify properties that haven't been specified. Additionally, the formal specifications themselves must be carefully reviewed to ensure they correctly capture intended behavior.

Performance considerations become important when implementing formal verification. Verification tools can require significant computational resources, especially for complex properties or large state spaces. Teams should establish appropriate timeouts and resource limits for verification tasks and optimize specifications for verification performance.

Continuous verification ensures that formal guarantees remain valid as code evolves. This involves integrating verification tools into continuous integration pipelines and establishing processes for updating and reverifying specifications when changes occur. Failed verifications should block deployments until issues are resolved.

The field of formal verification for smart contracts continues to evolve rapidly. New tools and techniques emerge regularly, offering improved automation, better performance, and support for more complex properties. Teams should stay informed about developments in this space and be prepared to adopt new approaches as they mature.

Regulatory requirements increasingly recognize the value of formal verification in critical systems. Some jurisdictions or platforms may begin requiring formal verification for certain types of smart contracts. Understanding and implementing formal verification capabilities positions teams to meet such requirements as they emerge.

The cost-benefit analysis of formal verification depends heavily on the specific context. For high-value contracts where bugs could have catastrophic consequences, the investment in formal verification is easily justified. For simpler or lower-stakes contracts, lighter-weight verification approaches might be more appropriate.

37. Documentation Best Practices

Documentation plays a vital role in the security and maintainability of smart contracts. Clear, comprehensive documentation ensures that developers, auditors, and users can understand the contract's functionality, security measures, and intended behavior. This understanding is crucial for preventing misuse, facilitating maintenance, and enabling effective security reviews.

Smart contract documentation should begin with a high-level overview that explains the contract's purpose, main components, and key interactions. This overview helps readers quickly grasp the system's architecture and primary use cases. It should include diagrams illustrating contract relationships, data flows, and state transitions, making complex interactions more accessible to both technical and non-technical stakeholders.

Technical documentation must cover all public interfaces thoroughly. Each function should be documented with its purpose, parameters, return values, and any preconditions or postconditions. Special attention should be paid to documenting security-critical aspects such as access controls, value validation, and state modifications. Including examples of correct usage helps prevent integration errors and misunderstandings.

Internal documentation within the code itself is equally important. Comments should explain complex logic, mathematical formulas, and business rules that might not be immediately apparent from the code alone. However, comments should focus on explaining why certain decisions were made rather than merely restating what the code does. This context helps future maintainers understand the rationale behind implementation choices.

Security considerations deserve dedicated documentation sections. These should detail potential risks, implemented safeguards, and any assumptions about the operating environment. Documentation should explicitly state trust boundaries, describing which parts of the system trust which other parts and under what conditions. This information is crucial for security reviews and helps prevent misuse of the contract.

State machine documentation is particularly important for complex contracts. Clear descriptions of valid state transitions, including preconditions and postconditions for each state change, help prevent logical errors. State diagrams and transition tables make this information more accessible and help validate implementation correctness.

Error handling documentation should comprehensively cover all possible error conditions and their handling mechanisms. This includes describing error codes, revert messages, and the expected behavior when errors occur. Documentation should also explain how users and integrating systems should handle various error conditions.

Gas optimization strategies implemented in the contract should be documented to help users understand performance characteristics and cost implications. This includes explaining any batching mechanisms, storage patterns, or computational optimizations. Users need this information to effectively estimate transaction costs and optimize their interactions with the contract.

Version control documentation helps track changes and maintain backward compatibility. Each version should have clear release notes describing changes, especially those affecting security or backward compatibility. Documentation should explain upgrade paths and any migration steps required when moving between versions.

Testing documentation should describe the test suite's coverage, including both unit tests and integration tests. This helps maintainers understand what scenarios are already tested and where additional testing might be needed. Test documentation should also explain how to run tests and add new test cases.

Deployment documentation is crucial for ensuring consistent and secure contract deployment. This should include deployment prerequisites, configuration parameters, and verification steps. Documentation should also cover any initialization requirements and post-deployment validation procedures.

Integration guidelines help other developers correctly interact with the contract. These should include code examples, common integration patterns, and anti-patterns to avoid. Documentation should cover both direct contract interactions and events that other systems might need to monitor.

Emergency procedures should be clearly documented, including steps for handling security incidents, bug fixes, and contract upgrades. This documentation should specify roles and responsibilities during emergencies and include contact information for key stakeholders.

Monitoring requirements should be documented to help operators maintain system health. This includes describing important metrics, expected ranges, and recommended alerting thresholds. Documentation should also cover any automated monitoring tools or scripts provided with the contract.

User documentation needs to be accessible to non-technical stakeholders while still providing accurate information about contract behavior. This might include guides for common operations, explanations of key concepts, and troubleshooting information. Clear user documentation helps prevent operational errors and reduces support requirements.

Regulatory compliance documentation may be necessary depending on the contract's use case. This should detail how the contract addresses relevant regulatory requirements and any compliance-related features or restrictions. Documentation should also cover any reporting or audit trail requirements.

Architecture decisions and their rationales should be documented to preserve institutional knowledge. This includes explaining why particular patterns or approaches were chosen over alternatives. Such documentation helps future maintainers understand the context of implementation decisions and evaluate potential changes.

Performance characteristics should be documented to help users understand system limitations and optimization opportunities. This includes describing computational complexity, storage requirements, and any performance tradeoffs in the implementation. Users need this information to build efficient integrations.

Documentation maintenance procedures should be established to ensure documentation remains accurate as the contract evolves. This includes processes for reviewing and updating documentation during code changes, as well as regular reviews to identify and correct outdated information.

The documentation process itself should be documented, including style guides, templates, and tools used for documentation generation. This helps maintain consistency across documentation and makes it easier for team members to contribute documentation updates.

Language considerations are important when documenting contracts used internationally. Documentation should use clear, unambiguous language and avoid colloquialisms that might not translate well. Consider providing documentation in multiple languages for critical information.

Documentation should be treated as a critical project deliverable, not an afterthought. Teams should allocate appropriate time and resources for documentation creation and maintenance throughout the development lifecycle. Regular reviews should verify documentation completeness and accuracy.

38. Code Review Guidelines

Code review is a critical process in secure smart contract development that helps identify potential vulnerabilities, improve code quality, and ensure adherence to best practices. A systematic approach to code review can catch issues early in the development cycle, significantly reducing the risk of security incidents and costly fixes after deployment.

When conducting a code review for smart contracts, reviewers should first understand the contract's purpose and architecture. This includes reviewing the technical documentation, understanding the intended functionality, and identifying critical security requirements. A clear understanding of the context helps reviewers focus on relevant security considerations and potential edge cases.

The review process should begin with an automated analysis using static analysis tools and linters. These tools can quickly identify common issues like unused variables, inconsistent styling, and potential gas optimization opportunities. However, automated tools should be considered only as a first line of defense, complementing rather than replacing manual review.

Security-critical components deserve extra scrutiny during review. This includes access control mechanisms, value transfer functions, and state-changing operations. Reviewers should verify that proper access controls are in place, input validation is thorough, and state changes follow the expected business logic. Special attention should be paid to functions handling tokens or ether.

Reviewing mathematical operations requires particular care. Reviewers should verify that operations are protected against overflow and underflow, and that precision loss is handled appropriately. The use of safe math libraries should be confirmed, and complex calculations should be validated against test cases covering edge conditions.

Gas optimization should be evaluated during code review, but not at the expense of security or readability. Reviewers should look for unnecessary operations, inefficient storage patterns, and opportunities for batching. However, any optimization suggestions should be balanced against maintainability and security considerations.

External contract interactions require careful review to prevent vulnerabilities like reentrancy attacks. Reviewers should verify that the checks-effects-interactions pattern is followed, trust assumptions are clearly documented, and failure modes are properly handled. The review should consider both direct and indirect interactions through inherited contracts or libraries.

Event emission should be reviewed for completeness and correctness. Events provide important audit trails and enable external systems to track contract state changes. Reviewers should verify that events contain sufficient information for monitoring and that sensitive information is not inadvertently exposed.

Error handling implementation should be reviewed for consistency and completeness. This includes verifying that error messages are clear and helpful, revert conditions are appropriate, and error handling doesn't introduce security vulnerabilities. Custom error types should be reviewed for gas efficiency and clarity.

Code modularity and reusability should be evaluated during review. Reviewers should look for opportunities to reduce code duplication, improve separation of concerns, and enhance maintainability. However, suggested refactoring should consider the gas cost implications and potential security impacts.

Inheritance hierarchies require careful review to ensure proper function overriding and interface implementation. Reviewers should verify that contract interfaces are fully implemented, function visibility is appropriate, and inheritance doesn't introduce unexpected behavior or security vulnerabilities.

Storage layout deserves attention during review, particularly for upgradeable contracts. Reviewers should verify that storage slots are properly managed, storage patterns are gas efficient, and storage modifications don't risk data corruption during upgrades. Special attention should be paid to storage gaps in upgradeable contracts.

Access control implementations should be reviewed for completeness and correctness. This includes verifying role assignments, permission checks, and administrative functions. Reviewers should ensure that privilege escalation is not possible and that administrative functions have appropriate security controls.

Test coverage should be evaluated during code review. Reviewers should verify that tests cover critical paths, edge cases, and error conditions. Test quality is as important as quantity; tests should validate both positive and negative scenarios and include appropriate assertions.

Documentation quality should be assessed during review. Comments should be clear, accurate, and provide value beyond what's obvious from the code. NatSpec comments should be complete and correct, particularly for public interfaces. Documentation of security considerations and assumptions should be thorough.

Naming conventions and code organization should be reviewed for clarity and consistency. Clear, descriptive names help prevent misunderstandings that could lead to security issues. Code organization should follow project standards and make it easy to locate and understand different components.

Library usage should be reviewed for security implications. Reviewers should verify that external libraries are from trusted sources, properly audited, and appropriately versioned. The integration of libraries should be reviewed for correct usage and potential security impacts.

Upgradeability patterns, if used, require thorough review. This includes verifying proper implementation of proxy patterns, storage handling, and initialization logic. Reviewers should ensure that upgrades cannot lead to state corruption or security vulnerabilities.

State machine implementations should be reviewed for completeness and correctness. This includes verifying valid state transitions, proper access controls on state-changing functions, and appropriate event emissions for state changes. State machine logic should be clearly documented and tested.

Time-based logic requires careful review to ensure it handles edge cases appropriately. Reviewers should verify that time calculations are correct, block timestamp usage is appropriate, and time-based conditions don't introduce security vulnerabilities.

Code reviews should be documented with clear, actionable feedback. Issues should be categorized by severity and include specific recommendations for improvement. Review documentation helps track issue resolution and provides valuable input for security audits.

The review process should include multiple rounds as needed, with issues being addressed and changes being re-reviewed until all concerns are resolved. A final review should verify that all identified issues have been properly addressed and that fixes haven't introduced new problems.

Regular code reviews throughout the development process help maintain code quality and security. Teams should establish clear review procedures, including checklists and guidelines, to ensure consistent and thorough reviews. Building a culture of constructive code review helps improve overall code quality and security awareness.

39. Audit Preparation

Audit preparation is a crucial phase in the smart contract development lifecycle that can significantly impact the success and security of your project. Proper preparation not only makes the audit process more efficient but also increases the likelihood of identifying and addressing potential vulnerabilities before they become critical issues.

The first step in audit preparation is ensuring comprehensive documentation. This includes detailed technical specifications, architecture diagrams, and thorough documentation of all smart contract functions and their intended behaviors. Documentation should clearly explain the business logic, security assumptions, trust models, and any specific implementation decisions that might not be immediately apparent from the code alone.

Before engaging with auditors, conduct a thorough internal review of your codebase. This involves running automated analysis tools, performing comprehensive testing, and conducting internal security reviews. Address any known issues and optimize the code where possible. The goal is to present auditors with the most polished version of your code, allowing them to focus on finding more subtle or complex vulnerabilities.

Test coverage is particularly important during audit preparation. Ensure that your test suite covers all critical paths and edge cases. Unit tests should verify individual function behaviors, while integration tests should validate interactions between different contract components. Include tests for failure scenarios and potential attack vectors. High test coverage demonstrates to auditors that you've thoroughly considered various scenarios and helps them validate their findings.

Implement logging and monitoring capabilities before the audit begins. Proper event emission helps auditors understand state changes and contract behaviors. Consider adding temporary debugging events during the audit process to aid in vulnerability analysis. However, ensure that any sensitive information is not exposed through events.

Prepare a clear description of your project's trust assumptions and security model. This includes documenting who has access to administrative functions, how upgrades are managed, and what security measures are in place to protect user assets. Clearly state any assumptions about external contracts, oracles, or other dependencies.

Create a comprehensive threat model that identifies potential attack vectors and risks. Consider various adversarial scenarios, including malicious users, compromised administrators, and front-running attacks. Document how your implementation addresses these threats and any remaining risks that need special attention during the audit.

Organize your codebase to facilitate the audit process. Use clear file structures, consistent naming conventions, and thorough inline documentation. Remove any unused code, commented-out sections, or temporary modifications. Ensure that the version of the code being audited matches your documentation and deployment plans.

Prepare a list of specific areas where you would like auditors to focus their attention. This might include complex mathematical calculations, novel implementation patterns, or security-critical functions. While auditors will conduct a comprehensive review, highlighting areas of particular concern helps ensure these receive appropriate scrutiny.

Document any known limitations or potential issues in your implementation. This includes gas optimization trade-offs, specific platform dependencies, or conscious decisions to deviate from common patterns. Being transparent about these aspects helps auditors provide more relevant and actionable feedback.

Consider the timing of your audit carefully. Schedule it when your code is feature-complete and stable, but leave enough time to address findings before your planned deployment. Rush jobs often lead to missed vulnerabilities or inadequate remediation of identified issues.

Prepare your development team to be responsive during the audit process. Auditors may need clarification on certain implementation details or assistance reproducing potential issues. Quick and thorough responses help maintain audit momentum and ensure more comprehensive coverage.

Create a clear process for tracking and addressing audit findings. This includes procedures for evaluating the severity of issues, prioritizing fixes, and validating remediation measures. Consider how you will handle different types of findings, from critical vulnerabilities to gas optimization suggestions.

Document your deployment procedures and post-deployment monitoring plans. Auditors often provide recommendations for secure deployment practices and ongoing monitoring requirements. Having these procedures documented helps demonstrate your commitment to security beyond the initial audit.

Prepare technical documentation for any custom tools or scripts used in your development process. This includes deployment scripts, testing frameworks, or analysis tools. Auditors may need to understand these tools to evaluate their impact on contract security.

Consider conducting preliminary security assessments with automated tools before the formal audit. Tools like Slither, Mythril, or Manticore can identify common issues and provide a baseline for security analysis. Document any false positives or known limitations of these tools.

Review previous audit reports of similar projects to understand common findings in your domain. This helps you proactively address typical vulnerabilities and demonstrates industry awareness to auditors. Document how you've incorporated lessons learned from these reports into your implementation.

Prepare a detailed description of your testing environment and procedures. This includes information about the development network, test accounts, and any special configurations needed to validate contract behavior. Clear testing documentation helps auditors reproduce and verify potential issues.

Document your upgrade procedures if your contracts are upgradeable. This includes details about proxy patterns, storage layouts, and initialization procedures. Auditors need to understand how upgrades will be managed to evaluate potential risks and recommend appropriate controls.

Create a clear timeline and scope for the audit. This includes defining which contracts are in scope, any specific exclusions, and expected deliverables. Clear scope definition helps ensure efficient use of audit resources and comprehensive coverage of critical components.

Consider preparing a bug bounty program to complement the formal audit. Document your plans for ongoing security validation and how you will handle vulnerability reports after deployment. This demonstrates a long-term commitment to security and helps auditors understand your risk management approach.

The key to successful audit preparation is thoroughness and transparency. By providing comprehensive documentation, maintaining high code quality, and demonstrating security awareness, you enable auditors to conduct more effective reviews and provide more valuable recommendations for improving your smart contract security.

40. Common Audit Findings

Common audit findings represent recurring patterns of vulnerabilities and issues that security auditors frequently encounter during smart contract reviews. Understanding these common findings helps developers proactively address potential security concerns and build more robust smart contracts from the outset.

Access control vulnerabilities consistently rank among the most frequent audit findings. These often manifest as missing or incorrectly implemented permission checks, allowing unauthorized users to execute privileged functions. A common pattern involves administrative functions that lack proper ownership validation or rely on weak access control mechanisms. Auditors frequently discover functions intended to be restricted that are accidentally left public or protected by insufficient validation logic.

Reentrancy vulnerabilities remain a persistent concern despite being well documented. While developers are generally aware of direct reentrancy attacks, auditors often uncover more subtle variants involving cross function reentrancy or cross contract reentrancy. These vulnerabilities typically arise from inconsistent state management or failure to follow the checks effects interactions pattern. Particularly in DeFi protocols, complex token interactions create opportunities for reentrancy that may not be immediately apparent.

Integer overflow and underflow issues continue to appear in audit reports, especially in contracts that don't use SafeMath or Solidity versions prior to 0.8.0. These vulnerabilities often lurk in complex mathematical calculations, token economics implementations, or fee calculations. Auditors frequently identify edge cases where extreme values can cause unexpected behavior due to integer arithmetic limitations.

Gas optimization issues, while not strictly security vulnerabilities, are commonly flagged during audits. These include inefficient storage patterns, unnecessary storage reads and writes, unoptimized loops, and redundant calculations. Auditors often identify opportunities to reduce gas costs through better state variable packing, strategic use of memory versus storage, and optimization of frequently called functions.

Timestamp manipulation vulnerabilities are regularly discovered in contracts that rely on block timestamps for critical logic. This includes time locked functions, interest calculations, and random number generation. Auditors frequently highlight the potential for miners to manipulate timestamps within certain bounds and recommend more robust time management approaches.

Oracle related vulnerabilities constitute another common category of findings. These often involve insufficient validation of oracle data, lack of fallback mechanisms for oracle failures, or inadequate protection against price manipulation. Auditors typically identify scenarios where malicious actors could exploit oracle dependencies to manipulate contract behavior.

Event emission issues are frequently noted in audit reports. These include missing events for significant state changes, insufficient event parameters for proper monitoring, or inconsistent event emission patterns. While not always security critical, proper event emission is crucial for contract monitoring and frontend integration.

Upgrade related vulnerabilities are common in contracts implementing upgradeability patterns. Auditors often identify storage collision risks, initialization vulnerabilities, and function selector clashing. Implementation errors in proxy patterns or incomplete storage layouts can lead to serious vulnerabilities during contract upgrades.

Race condition vulnerabilities frequently appear in contracts handling multiple user interactions or external calls. These include front running opportunities, transaction ordering dependencies, and inconsistent state management across multiple transactions. DeFi protocols are particularly susceptible to these issues due to their complex interaction patterns.

Input validation vulnerabilities remain surprisingly common. These include missing or insufficient validation of function parameters, array lengths, or external contract addresses. Auditors regularly identify scenarios where malicious inputs could cause unexpected behavior or resource exhaustion.

Denial of service vulnerabilities often emerge from poorly implemented loops, unbounded operations, or inadequate gas management. These findings typically involve functions that could become unusable due to gas limitations or malicious user behavior. Particularly concerning are scenarios where critical contract functionality could be permanently blocked.

Business logic vulnerabilities represent a significant category of findings that go beyond technical implementation issues. These often involve unintended consequences of legitimate contract interactions or economic incentive misalignments. Auditors frequently identify ways that rational actors could exploit contract mechanics in unexpected ways.

Error handling deficiencies are commonly identified during audits. These include inconsistent error handling patterns, silent failures, or inadequate error reporting. Proper error handling is crucial for contract reliability and debugging capability.

Initialization vulnerabilities frequently appear in constructors or initialization functions. These include missing initialization checks, inadequate parameter validation, or opportunities for front running during contract deployment. Proper initialization is crucial for contract security but often overlooked.

Documentation inconsistencies are regularly highlighted in audit reports. These include discrepancies between code comments and implementation, unclear function purposes, or missing explanations for critical design decisions. While not direct vulnerabilities, documentation issues can lead to maintenance problems and security misunderstandings.

Token integration vulnerabilities are particularly common in DeFi protocols. These include insufficient handling of non standard tokens, missing token approval checks, or inadequate protection against fee on transfer tokens. Auditors frequently identify scenarios where unusual token behavior could disrupt contract operation.

State management vulnerabilities often involve inconsistent state updates, missing state validation, or improper handling of edge cases. These findings typically relate to complex state transitions or interactions between multiple state variables.

External contract interaction vulnerabilities remain a persistent concern. These include insufficient validation of external calls, missing return value checks, or inadequate protection against malicious contracts. Auditors regularly identify ways that malicious external contracts could exploit trust assumptions.

Privacy leakage findings are increasingly common as privacy considerations become more important. These include unintended exposure of sensitive information through events, state variables, or transaction data. While not always critical security issues, privacy leakages can have significant implications for certain applications.

Understanding these common audit findings helps developers implement more secure contracts from the start and prepare more effectively for security audits. Regular review of public audit reports and security best practices remains crucial for staying current with evolving security concerns in smart contract development.

41. Deployment Security

Deployment security represents a critical phase in the smart contract development lifecycle where many projects encounter significant vulnerabilities. The deployment process requires careful preparation, precise execution, and robust verification to ensure the secure launch of smart contracts on the blockchain.

The deployment preparation phase begins with a comprehensive review of all contract dependencies and initialization parameters. Developers must carefully validate all constructor arguments, initial state variables, and configuration settings. This includes verifying administrative addresses, token addresses, protocol parameters, and any other deployment constants. A common pitfall involves hardcoding test values or placeholder addresses that accidentally make it into production deployments.

Contract verification on block explorers like Etherscan represents an essential security practice. Verified source code allows users and auditors to inspect the deployed contract implementation and compare it with the audited codebase. The verification process should include all contract dependencies and libraries. Developers should maintain careful records of compiler versions, optimization settings, and other compilation parameters to ensure successful verification.

Deployment scripts require particular attention to security. These scripts should implement comprehensive error handling, validation checks, and deployment confirmation steps. Many projects benefit from implementing dry run functionality that simulates the deployment process without committing transactions. This allows verification of gas estimates, parameter validation, and deployment sequencing without risking actual funds or contract deployment.

The initialization sequence of complex contract systems demands careful orchestration. Many vulnerabilities arise from improper initialization order or missing initialization steps. Developers should implement deployment scripts that handle the entire initialization sequence atomically where possible, or include robust verification steps between initialization phases. This includes setting up proper permissions, configuring protocol parameters, and validating initial state.

Time locks and deployment delays can provide additional security during the deployment process. Some projects implement mandatory waiting periods between contract deployment and protocol activation. This allows time for final verification and provides opportunities to catch potential issues before the system becomes fully operational. These delay mechanisms can be particularly valuable for high value systems or contracts handling significant assets.

Gas management during deployment requires careful consideration. Complex contract deployments can involve significant gas costs and multiple transactions. Deployment scripts should implement proper gas estimation and include mechanisms to handle failed transactions or network congestion. Some projects implement staged deployments to manage gas costs and reduce the risk of failed deployments.

Post deployment verification represents a crucial security step. This includes automated testing of the deployed contracts, verification of initialization parameters, and validation of system state. Many projects implement dedicated post deployment verification scripts that exercise key contract functionality and verify expected behavior. This should include validation of access controls, state variables, and critical system parameters.

Contract upgradeability considerations significantly impact deployment security. Upgradeable contracts require careful handling of implementation contracts, proxy contracts, and initialization logic. Developers must verify proper storage layouts, implementation addresses, and upgrade permissions. The deployment process should include specific steps to validate upgradeability mechanics and ensure proper initialization of upgradeable components.

Network specific considerations play a crucial role in deployment security. Different networks may have varying characteristics that affect deployment, such as gas costs, block times, or network specific quirks. Deployment scripts should account for these differences and implement appropriate network specific logic. This includes handling different network configurations, gas prices, and confirmation times.

Deployment key management represents a critical security concern. The accounts used for contract deployment often retain special privileges or administrative access. Proper key management procedures, including hardware wallets or multi signature schemes, should be implemented for deployment accounts. Some projects implement specific deployment roles that are transferred or renounced after initial setup.

Documentation of the deployment process serves both security and maintenance purposes. Detailed deployment records should include contract addresses, transaction hashes, initialization parameters, and any issues encountered during deployment. This documentation proves invaluable for future upgrades, troubleshooting, or security investigations.

Emergency procedures should be established before deployment. These include plans for handling failed deployments, addressing initialization issues, or responding to discovered vulnerabilities. Some projects implement specific emergency functions that can be activated during the deployment phase if issues are discovered.

Monitoring systems should be activated as part of the deployment process. This includes setting up alerts for significant events, monitoring transaction activity, and tracking key protocol metrics. Early detection of potential issues during and immediately after deployment can prevent or minimize security incidents.

Front end integration security requires careful consideration during deployment. This includes updating contract addresses, verifying ABI consistency, and validating interaction patterns. Many security incidents occur due to mismatches between deployed contracts and front end implementations.

The deployment environment itself requires security consideration. This includes securing deployment machines, protecting deployment scripts, and maintaining careful control over deployment parameters and secrets. Many projects implement specific deployment environments with enhanced security controls and limited access.

Community communication represents an often overlooked aspect of deployment security. Clear communication about deployment status, verification steps, and initialization processes helps prevent user confusion and potential security issues. Some projects implement specific deployment monitoring pages or status updates to keep stakeholders informed.

Regulatory compliance considerations may affect deployment procedures. This includes implementing required delays, obtaining necessary approvals, or meeting specific regulatory requirements. Deployment scripts and procedures should account for any compliance related requirements or restrictions.

Long term maintenance considerations should influence deployment procedures. This includes implementing proper logging, maintaining deployment records, and establishing update procedures. The deployment process should establish foundations for ongoing maintenance and future updates.

Human error remains a significant risk during deployment. Implementation of proper review procedures, deployment checklists, and validation steps helps minimize this risk. Many projects benefit from having multiple team members verify deployment steps and parameters before execution.

The deployment phase represents a critical security moment in a smart contract's lifecycle. Careful attention to deployment security helps ensure successful launch and ongoing operation of blockchain applications. Regular review and updating of deployment procedures remains essential as the ecosystem evolves and new security considerations emerge.

42. Network-Specific Considerations

Network-specific considerations play a vital role in smart contract security and deployment strategy. Different blockchain networks, even those that are EVM-compatible, possess unique characteristics, limitations, and security implications that developers must carefully consider during development and deployment.

The Ethereum mainnet presents distinct challenges compared to test networks or other EVM chains. Gas costs on mainnet are significantly higher, making optimization crucial for deployment and user interaction. Network congestion can impact transaction confirmation times and potentially affect contract functionality. Developers must implement robust handling of these network-specific characteristics, including appropriate gas price strategies and transaction timeout mechanisms.

Layer 2 solutions and sidechains introduce additional complexity to network considerations. These networks may have different block times, gas token mechanisms, or consensus rules that affect contract behavior. For example, Polygon's faster block times might require adjusting timeout parameters or reconsideration of time-based logic. Optimistic rollups like Arbitrum and Optimism introduce unique challenges with cross-chain message passing and fraud proof windows that must be accounted for in contract design.

Different networks may implement varying versions of the EVM or include network-specific opcodes and precompiles. Developers must ensure their contracts remain compatible across target networks and carefully test network-specific features. Some networks might offer additional precompiled contracts or special functions that can be leveraged for optimization, but these must be used cautiously to maintain cross-network compatibility when required.

Gas token mechanisms vary significantly across networks. While Ethereum uses ETH for gas payments, other networks might use native tokens or implement different fee structures. Smart contracts designed to handle gas refunds or implement gas tokenization strategies must account for these differences. Some networks implement different gas price mechanisms or fee markets that affect optimal transaction strategies.

Network security characteristics vary significantly. The level of decentralization, validator set size, and consensus mechanisms affect the security assumptions that can be made. For example, contracts deployed on networks with smaller validator sets might need additional confirmation blocks before considering transactions final. Some networks might be more susceptible to block reorganizations, requiring careful consideration of confirmation times and finality assumptions.

Cross-chain functionality introduces complex network-specific considerations. Bridges between networks often implement different security models and trust assumptions. Contracts designed to interact with bridge protocols must carefully handle network-specific bridge implementations and potential failure modes. Some networks implement native cross-chain communication protocols that require specific handling in contract logic.

Network upgrades and hard forks require careful consideration. Different networks may implement protocol upgrades at different times or choose not to implement certain EIPs. Contracts must remain compatible with planned network upgrades and implement appropriate fallback mechanisms for networks that may not support certain features. This includes careful handling of deprecated opcodes and potential changes to gas costs or execution rules.

Testing strategies must account for network-specific characteristics. Development teams should implement comprehensive testing across all target networks, including mainnet forks and network-specific test environments. This includes testing under various network conditions, such as high congestion or volatile gas prices, and validating network-specific features and limitations.

Network-specific development tools and infrastructure require consideration. Different networks may offer varying levels of development support, including block explorers, debugging tools, or infrastructure services. Contracts should implement appropriate fallback mechanisms when certain services are unavailable on specific networks. This includes handling differences in RPC endpoint behavior or block explorer APIs.

Oracle implementations often require network-specific consideration. Different networks may have varying levels of oracle support or implement different oracle protocols. Contracts relying on oracle data must handle network-specific oracle implementations and potential differences in data availability or update frequencies. Some networks might require implementing custom oracle solutions or adapting existing oracle integrations.

Network-specific token standards and implementations need careful handling. While most networks follow similar token standards, implementation details and common practices might vary. Contracts interacting with tokens must account for these differences and implement appropriate validation and handling mechanisms. This includes careful consideration of decimals, transfer mechanisms, and potential token-specific behaviors.

Front-running protection strategies may need network-specific adjustment. Different networks have varying block times and mining/validation mechanisms that affect the feasibility of front-running attacks. Solutions like commit-reveal schemes or flash bots might need adaptation for specific network characteristics. Some networks might offer native front-running protection mechanisms that can be leveraged.

Error handling and recovery mechanisms should consider network-specific failure modes. Different networks might have varying transaction reversion behaviors or error reporting mechanisms. Contracts should implement robust error handling that accounts for network-specific characteristics and provides appropriate recovery mechanisms. This includes handling network-specific transaction failures and implementing appropriate retry logic.

Monitoring and alerting systems require network-specific configuration. Different networks may require varying approaches to monitoring transaction status, event logging, or error detection. Teams should implement appropriate monitoring solutions for each target network and establish network-specific alert thresholds and response procedures.

Documentation should clearly specify network-specific requirements and limitations. This includes detailing supported networks, network-specific configuration requirements, and any features that may behave differently across networks. Clear documentation helps prevent deployment issues and ensures proper contract usage across different networks.

Network-specific security considerations extend beyond technical implementation to include economic and social factors. Different networks may have varying levels of economic activity, liquidity, or user bases that affect contract security assumptions. Contracts handling significant value should carefully consider the security implications of deployment on different networks and implement appropriate safeguards.

43. Front-Running Prevention

Front running has become one of the most significant challenges in decentralized applications, particularly in decentralized exchanges and other high-value transaction systems. This chapter explores comprehensive strategies and patterns for preventing front running attacks while maintaining contract efficiency and usability.

Front running occurs when an attacker observes a pending transaction in the mempool and submits their own transaction with a higher gas price to ensure it gets processed first. This exploitation of transaction ordering can lead to significant financial losses and undermines the fairness of decentralized systems. Understanding the mechanics of front running is crucial for implementing effective prevention strategies.

The most basic form of front running protection involves implementing commit reveal schemes. In this pattern, users first submit a cryptographic commitment of their intended action, followed by a reveal transaction that executes the actual operation. This approach prevents attackers from knowing the exact nature of the transaction they're trying to front run. However, this solution comes with increased gas costs and complexity due to the requirement for multiple transactions.

Time-based protections can help mitigate front running risks. By implementing minimum waiting periods between transaction submissions or using block numbers as timing mechanisms, contracts can reduce the window of opportunity for front running attacks. However, developers must carefully balance security requirements with user experience, as excessive waiting periods can discourage legitimate users.

Batch auction mechanisms provide another approach to front running prevention. Instead of processing transactions immediately, the contract collects orders over a period and executes them in a single batch. This approach can include price finding mechanisms that ensure fair execution prices for all participants. The challenge lies in designing efficient batch processing logic while maintaining gas efficiency and managing the complexity of order matching.

Gas price limits and dynamic fee adjustments can help prevent certain types of front running attacks. By implementing maximum gas price limits or requiring consistent gas prices across related transactions, contracts can reduce the ability of attackers to manipulate transaction ordering. However, these mechanisms must be carefully designed to remain effective during periods of network congestion.

Private mempool solutions, such as Flashbots, offer another avenue for front running prevention. These systems allow transactions to be submitted directly to miners, bypassing the public mempool where they could be observed by attackers. While effective, this approach requires specific infrastructure support and may not be available on all networks.

Zero knowledge proofs present an advanced solution for front running prevention. By allowing users to prove they have a valid transaction without revealing its details, zero knowledge systems can prevent attackers from identifying profitable front running opportunities. However, implementing zero knowledge systems adds significant complexity and computational overhead.

Order matching engines can be designed with front running resistance in mind. By implementing fair ordering mechanisms and price finding algorithms that are resistant to manipulation, contracts can reduce the impact of front running attempts. This might include using time-weighted average prices or implementing price impact calculations that make front running less profitable.

Slippage protection mechanisms are essential for preventing front running in trading systems. By allowing users to specify maximum slippage limits and implementing proper price validation, contracts can protect users from excessive price manipulation. These mechanisms should be carefully tuned to balance protection against legitimate price movements.

MEV (Miner Extractable Value) resistant designs can help prevent more sophisticated forms of front running. This includes implementing mechanisms that reduce the profitability of sandwich attacks and other MEV extraction strategies. Developers should consider how their contract's economic design might create opportunities for MEV extraction and implement appropriate countermeasures.

Decentralized price oracles must be carefully implemented to prevent front running through price manipulation. This includes using time weighted average prices, multiple data sources, and appropriate update mechanisms. Contracts should implement circuit breakers and other safety mechanisms to prevent exploitation of oracle data.

Transaction ordering independence is a powerful design pattern for preventing front running. By designing contract logic that produces the same result regardless of transaction ordering, developers can eliminate many front running opportunities. However, this approach may not be feasible for all applications and requires careful consideration of contract state management.

Monitoring and detection systems play a crucial role in front running prevention. By implementing proper logging and monitoring mechanisms, teams can detect potential front running attempts and adjust their prevention strategies accordingly. This includes monitoring for suspicious transaction patterns and implementing appropriate alert systems.

Gas efficiency remains important when implementing front running prevention mechanisms. Complex prevention strategies can significantly increase gas costs, potentially making the contract unusable during high gas price periods. Developers must carefully balance security requirements with gas optimization.

Testing front running prevention mechanisms requires specialized approaches. This includes simulating various attack scenarios, testing under different network conditions, and validating the effectiveness of prevention mechanisms. Teams should implement comprehensive testing suites that cover both normal operation and potential attack vectors.

Documentation of front running prevention mechanisms should be clear and comprehensive. This includes explaining the security assumptions, limitations, and proper usage of prevention mechanisms. Users should understand the protections in place and any required actions on their part to maintain security.

Front running prevention remains an active area of research and development in the blockchain space. New prevention mechanisms and best practices continue to emerge as the understanding of front running attacks evolves. Development teams should stay informed about new developments and be prepared to adapt their prevention strategies as needed.

44. Secure Key Management

Secure key management forms the foundation of blockchain security, serving as a critical element in protecting smart contracts and the assets they control. This chapter explores comprehensive approaches to managing private keys, contract ownership, and access credentials in decentralized applications.

Private key management represents one of the most crucial aspects of smart contract security. The loss or compromise of private keys can lead to catastrophic consequences, including complete loss of contract control and potential theft of assets. Implementing robust key management systems requires careful consideration of storage mechanisms, access patterns, and recovery procedures.

Smart contracts often implement ownership patterns that rely on private keys for administrative control. The standard Ownable pattern, while useful for simple applications, may not provide sufficient security for high value contracts. Advanced key management systems should implement multiple layers of security, including time locks, multi signature requirements, and graduated access controls based on key hierarchy.

Cold storage solutions play a vital role in secure key management for smart contracts. Critical private keys, particularly those controlling administrative functions or large amounts of value, should be stored in offline systems isolated from network access. This might involve hardware security modules, air gapped computers, or specialized key management infrastructure designed for institutional use.

Key rotation mechanisms provide an important security feature for long lived contracts. By allowing controlled changes of critical keys while maintaining security invariants, contracts can reduce the risk of key compromise and adapt to changing security requirements. Implementation of key rotation must carefully consider access controls, timing constraints, and proper validation of rotation requests.

Multi signature schemes form a cornerstone of secure key management in enterprise applications. By requiring multiple independent signatures for critical operations, contracts can prevent single points of failure and enforce separation of duties. Implementation considerations include threshold selection, key holder designation, and efficient signature verification mechanisms.

Recovery mechanisms must be carefully designed to handle key loss scenarios without introducing new vulnerabilities. This might include social recovery systems, backup key sets, or timelocked recovery procedures. Each recovery mechanism should be thoroughly tested and documented, with clear procedures for verification and execution.

Hardware security modules (HSMs) provide an additional layer of protection for critical keys. Integration with HSMs requires careful consideration of interface requirements, performance implications, and backup procedures. Contracts should be designed to work efficiently with HSM signing delays while maintaining security properties.

Key generation procedures form a critical part of the security lifecycle. Implementing secure random number generation, proper entropy sources, and validated key derivation functions ensures the fundamental security of the key management system. Documentation should include detailed procedures for secure key generation and validation.

Access control systems must be designed to work seamlessly with key management infrastructure. This includes implementing proper role based access control, managing key permissions, and maintaining audit logs of key usage. Systems should support fine grained control over key capabilities while remaining gas efficient.

Time locked operations provide an additional security layer for key management. By implementing mandatory delay periods for critical operations, contracts can provide opportunity for monitoring and intervention in case of key compromise. These mechanisms must balance security requirements with operational flexibility.

Monitoring systems play a crucial role in key management security. Implementing comprehensive logging of key usage, automated alerts for suspicious activities, and regular audit procedures helps maintain the security of the key management system. Monitoring should cover both on chain and off chain components of the system.

Backup procedures must be carefully designed and tested to ensure continuity of operations. This includes secure storage of backup keys, documented recovery procedures, and regular testing of recovery mechanisms. Organizations should maintain multiple secure copies of critical keys while ensuring they remain protected from unauthorized access.

Integration with external key management services requires careful consideration of security boundaries and trust assumptions. When utilizing third party key management services, contracts should implement proper validation and fallback mechanisms while maintaining security properties. Documentation should clearly specify dependencies and operational requirements.

Gas optimization remains important when implementing key management features. Complex signature verification, multi signature schemes, and key rotation mechanisms can significantly impact gas costs. Implementations should carefully balance security requirements with operational efficiency.

Environmental security plays a crucial role in key management. Physical security measures, access controls, and proper operational procedures must be maintained to protect key management systems. Documentation should include detailed security requirements for key management infrastructure.

Testing key management systems requires specialized approaches. This includes verification of cryptographic implementations, testing of recovery procedures, and validation of security properties under various failure scenarios. Teams should implement comprehensive testing suites covering both normal operations and edge cases.

Regulatory compliance often imposes specific requirements on key management systems. This might include requirements for key custody, audit trails, and specific security controls. Implementation should consider relevant regulatory frameworks and maintain appropriate documentation.

User education forms an important component of key management security. Users must understand their responsibilities in maintaining key security, proper usage patterns, and recovery procedures. Documentation should include clear guidelines for key handling and security best practices.

Key management systems must evolve with changing security requirements and threats. Regular security reviews, updates to security procedures, and adaptation to new best practices help maintain the effectiveness of key management systems. Teams should maintain awareness of emerging threats and security developments.

Integration with smart contract upgrades requires careful consideration of key management implications. This includes maintaining security during upgrade procedures, managing key transitions, and ensuring continuity of security properties. Documentation should clearly specify procedures for handling keys during contract upgrades.

The future of key management in smart contracts continues to evolve with new technologies and security requirements. Developments in areas such as quantum resistant cryptography, secure enclaves, and distributed key management systems may influence future implementations. Teams should maintain awareness of emerging technologies and their potential impact on key management security.

45. Error Handling Patterns

Error handling patterns represent a critical aspect of smart contract development that can mean the difference between graceful failure recovery and catastrophic loss of funds. Proper error handling ensures contracts behave predictably even when encountering unexpected conditions, while providing clear feedback about failure modes to users and monitoring systems.

Smart contracts must implement comprehensive error handling strategies that account for both expected and unexpected failure conditions. This includes proper use of require statements, revert operations, and custom error definitions. The pattern chosen should balance gas efficiency with clarity of error reporting, ensuring that failed operations provide sufficient information for debugging while maintaining reasonable execution costs.

Custom errors in Solidity provide a gas efficient mechanism for reporting specific failure conditions. By defining structured error types, contracts can communicate detailed information about failure modes while consuming less gas than traditional string error messages. Implementation should consider careful naming of error types, inclusion of relevant parameters, and clear documentation of error conditions.

Transaction reversion patterns must be carefully designed to maintain contract invariants. When operations fail, the contract should return to a consistent state without partial updates that could compromise security. This often involves implementing checks before state modifications, using appropriate control flow structures, and carefully ordering operations to maintain atomicity.

Exception handling in external calls requires special attention. The try catch pattern introduced in recent Solidity versions provides improved control over external call failures, allowing contracts to implement specific handling for different types of errors.

Implementation should consider gas implications, proper error propagation, and maintenance of contract invariants during error recovery.

Assertion based error handling serves an important role in contract development and testing. Strategic placement of assert statements helps identify logical errors and invariant violations during development, while providing additional safety checks in production. Implementation should balance the security benefits of assertions with their gas costs.

Error logging mechanisms provide crucial information for monitoring and debugging. Contracts should emit appropriate events when handling errors, providing sufficient detail for post mortem analysis while maintaining gas efficiency. Implementation should consider structured logging patterns, appropriate level of detail, and integration with monitoring systems.

Recovery procedures must be carefully designed to handle various error conditions. This includes implementing appropriate fallback mechanisms, providing clear paths for error recovery, and maintaining proper access controls over recovery operations. Documentation should clearly specify recovery procedures and their associated security implications.

Input validation forms a critical component of error handling. Contracts should implement comprehensive validation of all inputs, including parameter ranges, address validity, and semantic constraints. Implementation should provide clear error messages for validation failures while maintaining gas efficiency through appropriate validation ordering.

State management during error conditions requires careful consideration. Contracts should implement proper cleanup procedures when operations fail, ensuring no resources are leaked and the contract returns to a consistent state. This includes proper handling of partial operations, cleanup of temporary state, and maintenance of invariants.

Recursive call handling presents particular challenges for error management. Contracts must carefully handle errors in recursive operations, preventing stack overflow conditions while maintaining proper state consistency. Implementation should consider depth limits, proper error propagation, and gas implications of recursive operations.

Integration with external systems requires robust error handling patterns. Contracts should implement appropriate fallback mechanisms when external services fail, maintain proper state consistency, and provide clear error information for debugging. Implementation should consider timeout handling, retry mechanisms, and proper error propagation.

Gas management forms an important aspect of error handling. Contracts should implement appropriate gas checks before expensive operations, handle out of gas conditions gracefully, and provide clear feedback about gas related failures. Implementation should consider gas estimation, proper failure modes, and user feedback mechanisms.

Error handling in upgradeable contracts presents additional challenges. Implementation must consider error handling across contract versions, maintaining consistent error reporting patterns, and proper handling of initialization errors. Documentation should clearly specify error handling changes across contract versions.

Monitoring systems play a crucial role in error management. Contracts should implement comprehensive error logging, integrate with monitoring services, and provide appropriate alerts for critical errors. Implementation should consider log structuring, alert thresholds, and integration with operational procedures.

Testing error conditions requires specialized approaches. Implementation should include comprehensive testing of error paths, validation of error handling mechanisms, and verification of recovery procedures. Test suites should cover both expected and unexpected error conditions, ensuring proper handling across all failure modes.

User interface integration requires careful consideration of error handling. Contracts should provide clear, actionable error messages that can be properly interpreted and displayed by frontend applications. Implementation should consider error message localization, proper error code mapping, and user friendly error presentation.

Security implications of error handling must be carefully considered. Implementation should prevent information leakage through error messages, maintain proper access controls during error recovery, and prevent exploitation of error conditions. Documentation should clearly specify security considerations for error handling mechanisms.

Error handling patterns continue to evolve with the Solidity language and best practices. Teams should stay informed about new language features, emerging patterns, and security considerations related to error handling. Regular review and updates of error handling mechanisms help maintain robust and secure contracts.

Documentation plays a crucial role in error handling. Contracts should maintain clear documentation of error conditions, handling mechanisms, and recovery procedures. This includes proper inline code documentation, external specification documents, and operational procedures for handling various types of errors.

46. Secure Contract Migration

Smart contract migration represents a critical process in the lifecycle management of blockchain applications, requiring careful planning and execution to ensure security and continuity of operations. Successful migration strategies must account for data preservation, state management, and user experience while maintaining the highest security standards throughout the transition process.

The foundation of secure contract migration begins with comprehensive preparation. Development teams must thoroughly analyze existing contract deployments, identifying all dependencies, state variables, and external interactions that need to be preserved or updated during migration. This includes mapping out all contract relationships, documenting storage layouts, and understanding the full scope of potential impacts on users and integrated systems.

Data migration strategies form a crucial component of secure contract transitions. Teams must implement robust mechanisms for transferring state between contract versions, ensuring no critical information is lost or corrupted during the process. This often involves creating specialized migration contracts that handle state transfer in a systematic, verifiable manner while maintaining proper access controls throughout the process.

Storage layout compatibility requires particular attention during migration planning. Changes to storage layouts between contract versions can lead to serious issues if not properly managed. Teams must carefully document storage structures, implement appropriate storage gaps for future extensibility, and verify storage compatibility across contract versions to prevent data corruption during migration.

User communication plays a vital role in successful contract migration. Teams should implement clear notification mechanisms, provide detailed documentation of migration procedures, and ensure users understand any required actions. This includes appropriate timing of notifications, clear instructions for any necessary user interactions, and proper handling of user assets during the transition period.

Migration timing requires careful consideration to minimize disruption to users and integrated systems. Teams should plan migration windows during periods of lower activity, implement appropriate waiting periods for users to prepare, and ensure all stakeholders are properly notified of the migration schedule. This includes coordination with external dependencies and consideration of network conditions during the planned migration window.

Atomic migration patterns help ensure consistency during the transition process. When possible, migrations should be implemented as atomic operations that either completely succeed or fail, preventing partial migrations that could leave the system in an inconsistent state. This often involves implementing proper checkpoint mechanisms and rollback procedures for complex migrations.

State verification forms a critical component of secure migration. Teams must implement comprehensive verification procedures to ensure all state is correctly transferred and maintained during migration. This includes automated validation of critical state variables, user balances, and system parameters, with appropriate logging and monitoring throughout the process.

Access control during migration requires careful management. Teams must implement proper permissions for migration operations, ensuring only authorized parties can initiate and manage the migration process. This includes appropriate timelock mechanisms, multi signature requirements, and proper validation of migration parameters.

Testing migration procedures demands thorough preparation. Teams should implement comprehensive test suites that verify all aspects of the migration process, including state transfer, access controls, and error handling. This includes testing on appropriate test networks, simulation of various failure scenarios, and verification of all recovery procedures.

Gas optimization during migration requires careful consideration. Teams must implement efficient migration procedures that minimize gas costs while maintaining security. This includes proper batching of operations, optimization of state transfer mechanisms, and careful management of storage operations during migration.

Recovery procedures must be clearly defined for migration operations. Teams should implement appropriate fallback mechanisms, clear procedures for handling failed migrations, and proper documentation of recovery steps. This includes testing of recovery procedures, verification of rollback mechanisms, and clear documentation of emergency procedures.

Integration testing with external systems forms an important part of migration preparation. Teams must verify compatibility with all integrated services, ensure proper handling of external calls during migration, and maintain appropriate communication with dependent systems. This includes coordination with external teams, testing of integration points, and verification of system behavior post migration.

Monitoring systems play a crucial role during migration operations. Teams should implement comprehensive logging of migration steps, proper alerting for critical events, and clear visibility into migration progress. This includes appropriate metrics collection, real time monitoring of critical parameters, and proper integration with operational support systems.

Version management requires careful attention during migration. Teams must maintain clear versioning of contracts, proper documentation of changes between versions, and appropriate tracking of deployed contracts. This includes proper source control practices, clear changelog maintenance, and appropriate artifact management.

Security considerations must remain paramount throughout the migration process. Teams should implement appropriate security controls, maintain proper audit trails, and ensure all security properties are preserved during migration. This includes verification of security invariants, proper handling of sensitive data, and maintenance of access controls throughout the process.

Documentation plays a vital role in successful migration. Teams must maintain comprehensive documentation of migration procedures, clear specifications of all changes, and proper operational guides for executing migrations. This includes technical specifications, operational procedures, and user facing documentation.

Future proofing migration patterns helps ensure sustainable contract management. Teams should implement flexible migration mechanisms that can accommodate future changes, maintain proper extension points, and support evolving requirements. This includes appropriate use of proxy patterns, proper storage management, and maintainable code structures.

The success of contract migration ultimately depends on careful planning, thorough testing, and meticulous execution. Teams must balance the technical requirements of secure migration with practical operational considerations, ensuring smooth transitions while maintaining the highest security standards. Regular review and updates of migration procedures help maintain robust and secure contract management practices.

47. Version Control Best Practices

Version control represents a fundamental aspect of secure smart contract development, serving as the foundation for maintaining code quality, tracking changes, and enabling collaborative development while ensuring security throughout the development lifecycle. Proper version control practices not only facilitate team coordination but also provide crucial audit trails and help prevent security vulnerabilities from being introduced through code changes.

Git remains the predominant version control system in smart contract development, offering powerful features for managing source code and related assets. Teams should establish clear branching strategies that align with their development workflow while maintaining security considerations. The commonly adopted GitFlow model, with its separation of feature branches, development branches, and main branches, provides a solid foundation for secure development practices.

Branch protection rules form a critical component of secure version control practices. Teams should implement mandatory code review policies, requiring multiple approvals before changes can be merged into protected branches. This includes enabling branch protection settings that prevent force pushes, require status checks to pass before merging, and maintain a clean commit history through proper rebasing practices.

Commit signing adds an additional layer of security to version control practices. Teams should require cryptographic signing of commits using GPG keys, ensuring the authenticity and integrity of code changes. This practice helps prevent unauthorized code modifications and provides clear accountability for all changes to the codebase. Organizations should maintain proper key management procedures for developer signing keys and regularly verify the validity of signatures.

Semantic versioning plays a crucial role in managing smart contract releases. Teams should adopt clear versioning schemes that reflect the nature of changes, distinguishing between major updates that introduce breaking changes, minor updates that add backwards compatible features, and patches that fix bugs or security issues. This helps users and integrating systems understand the impact of updates and maintain appropriate compatibility measures.

Documentation of changes requires systematic approaches through version control. Teams should maintain detailed changelog files that document all modifications, including security relevant changes, new features, and bug fixes. This documentation should be maintained alongside the code in version control, ensuring it remains synchronized with the actual implementation and provides a clear history of changes for auditors and developers.

Dependencies management through version control demands careful attention. Teams should implement proper lockfile management, explicit versioning of all dependencies, and regular security audits of dependent packages. This includes maintaining accurate package manifests, implementing automated dependency scanning, and establishing clear procedures for updating dependencies while maintaining security.

Testing artifacts require proper version control practices. Teams should maintain comprehensive test suites alongside their code, ensuring all tests are version controlled and properly documented. This includes unit tests, integration tests, and security specific test cases, with clear documentation of test coverage and security validation procedures.

Configuration management through version control needs careful consideration. Teams should implement proper handling of configuration files, ensuring sensitive information is never committed to version control while maintaining appropriate templates and documentation for configuration management. This includes proper use of environment variables, secure credential management, and clear documentation of configuration requirements.

Build artifacts require systematic management in version control. Teams should maintain clear procedures for handling compiled contracts, deployment scripts, and other build outputs. This includes proper gitignore configurations, systematic artifact naming conventions, and clear documentation of build procedures.

Code review processes should be tightly integrated with version control practices. Teams should implement systematic review procedures, maintain proper documentation of review findings, and ensure all security relevant changes receive appropriate scrutiny. This includes proper use of pull request templates, systematic review checklists, and clear documentation of review decisions.

Automated checks should be integrated into the version control workflow. Teams should implement comprehensive CI/CD pipelines that automatically verify code quality, run security checks, and validate test coverage for all changes. This includes automated linting, security scanning, and compliance validation integrated directly into the version control process.

Branch management strategies should account for security considerations. Teams should implement clear procedures for handling security fixes, maintaining proper isolation of security sensitive changes, and ensuring appropriate review processes for security critical updates. This includes proper handling of hotfix branches, clear procedures for emergency updates, and appropriate documentation of security relevant changes.

Tagging practices play an important role in version control security. Teams should implement systematic tagging of releases, ensuring all deployed versions can be clearly identified and reproduced. This includes proper signing of tags, clear documentation of release contents, and maintenance of appropriate release notes.

Access control to version control systems requires careful management. Teams should implement proper permission structures, ensuring appropriate access levels for different team members and maintaining clear procedures for managing access changes. This includes regular review of access permissions, proper offboarding procedures, and clear documentation of access control policies.

History preservation represents a critical aspect of secure version control. Teams should maintain complete historical records of all changes, ensuring the ability to audit past modifications and understand the evolution of security relevant code. This includes proper handling of force push restrictions, maintenance of clear commit messages, and appropriate documentation of historical changes.

Integration with security tools should be managed through version control. Teams should maintain proper configuration of security scanning tools, ensure appropriate integration with vulnerability databases, and maintain clear procedures for handling security findings. This includes proper version control of security tool configurations, clear documentation of security processes, and appropriate tracking of security issues.

Backup procedures for version control systems require careful attention. Teams should implement proper backup strategies for their repositories, ensuring no critical information can be lost due to system failures or security incidents. This includes proper replication of repositories, regular backup validation, and clear recovery procedures.

The effectiveness of version control practices in maintaining security depends on consistent application and regular review of procedures. Teams should periodically assess their version control practices, update procedures based on lessons learned, and ensure all team members maintain proper security awareness in their use of version control systems. Regular training and updates to version control procedures help maintain robust security practices throughout the development lifecycle.

48. Continuous Integration for Smart Contracts

Continuous Integration (CI) plays a vital role in ensuring the security and reliability of smart contract development by automating crucial validation, testing, and deployment processes. A well implemented CI pipeline helps catch potential security vulnerabilities early, maintains consistent code quality, and ensures that all changes undergo proper validation before deployment.

Setting up a comprehensive CI pipeline for smart contract development requires careful consideration of the unique challenges posed by blockchain applications. The pipeline should include automated compilation and verification of contract code, comprehensive test execution, security analysis, gas optimization checks, and proper handling of deployment artifacts.

The foundation of any smart contract CI pipeline begins with automated build processes. Teams should implement automated compilation of contracts using consistent compiler versions, with proper validation of compilation outputs. This includes checking for compiler warnings, verifying bytecode generation, and ensuring consistent optimization settings across all builds. The pipeline should maintain proper artifacts from the build process, including both the compiled bytecode and generated ABIs.

Test automation forms a critical component of smart contract CI pipelines. The system should automatically execute all test suites, including unit tests, integration tests, and security specific test cases. This includes proper handling of test networks, management of test accounts, and validation of test coverage metrics. The pipeline should fail builds that don't meet predetermined test coverage thresholds or that introduce test failures.

Security scanning integration represents an essential aspect of smart contract CI pipelines. Teams should incorporate automated security analysis tools that can identify common vulnerabilities, check for known attack patterns, and validate security best practices. This includes integration with static analysis tools, automated vulnerability scanners, and custom security validation scripts. The pipeline should maintain clear reporting of security findings and fail builds that introduce potential security issues.

Gas optimization validation should be automated within the CI pipeline. This includes running gas usage analysis tools, comparing gas costs against established benchmarks, and identifying potential optimization opportunities. The pipeline should maintain historical gas usage metrics and alert on significant changes that might impact contract efficiency.

Contract size validation needs to be automated within the pipeline. This includes checking that compiled contracts remain within deployment size limits, validating optimization settings, and ensuring efficient code organization. The pipeline should fail builds that exceed size thresholds or that introduce unnecessary code bloat.

Dependency validation forms another crucial aspect of CI pipelines. The system should automatically verify all external dependencies, check for known vulnerabilities in dependent packages, and ensure consistent dependency versions across builds. This includes integration with dependency scanning tools and maintenance of proper dependency lockfiles.

Documentation validation should be integrated into the CI process. The pipeline should verify that all code changes include appropriate documentation updates, check for documentation completeness, and ensure consistent documentation formatting. This includes validation of NatSpec comments, verification of external documentation, and checking for proper change documentation.

Code style enforcement needs to be automated within the pipeline. Teams should implement automated linting and formatting checks that ensure consistent code style across the project. This includes validation of naming conventions, code organization patterns, and documentation standards. The pipeline should fail builds that don't meet established style guidelines.

Integration testing automation requires careful consideration in CI pipelines. The system should automatically deploy contracts to test networks, execute integration test suites, and validate contract interactions. This includes proper management of test network connections, handling of test account funding, and validation of cross contract communications.

Contract verification automation represents an important aspect of CI pipelines. The system should automatically generate and validate contract verification artifacts, ensuring that deployed contracts can be properly verified on block explorers. This includes maintenance of source code mappings, generation of verification metadata, and validation of verification success.

Environment management needs proper automation within CI pipelines. The system should handle different deployment environments, manage environment specific configurations, and ensure proper separation of concerns between environments. This includes proper handling of environment variables, secure management of deployment credentials, and validation of environment specific settings.

Artifact management requires systematic automation within the pipeline. The system should properly handle build artifacts, maintain consistent naming conventions, and ensure proper versioning of outputs. This includes management of compiled contracts, deployment scripts, and associated metadata.

Deployment automation forms a critical component of CI pipelines. Teams should implement automated deployment procedures that include proper validation steps, environment specific configurations, and rollback capabilities. This includes automated deployment to test networks, proper handling of deployment parameters, and validation of deployment success.

Performance testing automation should be integrated into the pipeline. The system should execute automated performance tests, validate gas usage patterns, and identify potential performance bottlenecks. This includes proper benchmarking of contract operations, validation of gas efficiency, and identification of optimization opportunities.

Reporting and notification systems need proper implementation within CI pipelines. The system should generate comprehensive build reports, maintain proper logging of all pipeline steps, and provide appropriate notifications of build status. This includes integration with communication tools, maintenance of build histories, and proper error reporting.

The effectiveness of CI pipelines depends heavily on proper monitoring and maintenance. Teams should regularly review pipeline performance, update automation scripts as needed, and ensure all team members understand proper pipeline usage. This includes regular validation of pipeline functionality, updates to automation tools, and maintenance of pipeline documentation.

Integration with development workflows requires careful consideration. The pipeline should properly handle different branch strategies, maintain appropriate triggers for different types of changes, and ensure proper validation based on change context. This includes proper handling of feature branches, maintenance of deployment environments, and appropriate validation levels for different change types.

The success of continuous integration in smart contract development relies on consistent application and regular refinement of automation processes. Teams should periodically review their CI practices, update automation based on lessons learned, and ensure all team members maintain proper understanding of pipeline usage. Regular updates to CI procedures help maintain robust security and quality practices throughout the development lifecycle.

49. Monitoring and Alerting Systems

Monitoring and alerting systems form a critical component of secure smart contract operations, providing real-time visibility into contract behavior and early warning of potential security issues. Implementing robust monitoring solutions helps teams maintain contract security, optimize performance, and respond quickly to emerging threats.

A comprehensive monitoring strategy begins with proper event logging within smart contracts. Contracts should emit well-structured events for all significant state changes, important operations, and security-relevant actions. These events serve as the foundation for monitoring systems, providing a detailed audit trail of contract activity and enabling real-time tracking of contract behavior.

Transaction monitoring represents a fundamental aspect of contract surveillance. Systems should track all incoming transactions, monitoring for unusual patterns, unexpected interactions, or potential attack signatures. This includes tracking transaction volumes, monitoring gas usage patterns, and identifying potentially malicious transaction sequences. Alerts should be configured for sudden spikes in transaction activity, unusual interaction patterns, or transactions from suspicious addresses.

State monitoring provides crucial insights into contract health. Systems should track key contract state variables, monitoring for unexpected changes, invalid states, or potential manipulation. This includes tracking balance changes, monitoring ownership transfers, and validating state transitions. Teams should implement alerts for unexpected state changes, invalid state combinations, or rapid state modifications that might indicate an attack.

Gas usage monitoring helps identify potential performance issues or attack attempts. Systems should track gas consumption patterns, monitoring for unusual spikes, inefficient operations, or potential denial of service attempts. This includes tracking average gas costs, monitoring for gas-intensive operations, and identifying transactions with abnormal gas usage. Alerts should be configured for significant deviations from expected gas patterns.

Balance monitoring forms an essential security control. Systems should track contract balances, monitoring for unexpected transfers, unusual withdrawal patterns, or potential fund drainage. This includes tracking both native currency and token balances, monitoring transfer patterns, and validating balance changes. Teams should implement alerts for large transfers, unusual withdrawal sequences, or rapid balance changes.

Interaction monitoring helps identify potential security issues in cross-contract communications. Systems should track external contract calls, monitoring for unexpected interactions, potential reentrancy attempts, or suspicious call patterns. This includes tracking call frequencies, monitoring call sequences, and validating return values. Alerts should be configured for unusual interaction patterns or potentially dangerous call combinations.

Error monitoring provides insights into contract operational health. Systems should track transaction failures, contract reverts, and error conditions, monitoring for unusual error patterns or potential attack attempts. This includes tracking error frequencies, monitoring error types, and identifying common failure patterns. Teams should implement alerts for unusual error rates or unexpected error conditions.

Access pattern monitoring helps identify potential security breaches. Systems should track function access patterns, monitoring for unauthorized attempts, unusual permission usage, or potential privilege escalation. This includes tracking administrative operations, monitoring permission changes, and validating access controls. Alerts should be configured for unauthorized access attempts or unusual permission modifications.

Network monitoring provides context for contract behavior. Systems should track network conditions, monitoring for potential network issues, unusual block reorganizations, or mining anomalies. This includes tracking block times, monitoring network congestion, and identifying potential network attacks. Teams should implement alerts for unusual network conditions that might affect contract security.

Dependency monitoring helps identify potential vulnerabilities in connected systems. Systems should track related contracts, monitoring for updates, potential compromises, or unexpected behavior in dependent systems. This includes tracking proxy implementations, monitoring oracle feeds, and validating external data sources. Alerts should be configured for changes in dependent systems or unusual behavior patterns.

Performance monitoring helps maintain efficient contract operations. Systems should track execution times, monitoring for performance degradation, unusual latency patterns, or potential bottlenecks. This includes tracking function execution times, monitoring cache effectiveness, and identifying performance issues. Teams should implement alerts for significant performance degradation or unusual execution patterns.

Security monitoring provides early warning of potential attacks. Systems should track known attack patterns, monitoring for suspicious activities, potential exploits, or emerging threats. This includes tracking common attack signatures, monitoring for new vulnerability patterns, and identifying potential security issues. Alerts should be configured for detected attack attempts or suspicious activity patterns.

Compliance monitoring helps maintain regulatory alignment. Systems should track compliance-related metrics, monitoring for potential violations, unusual patterns, or regulatory concerns. This includes tracking transaction limits, monitoring reporting requirements, and validating compliance controls. Teams should implement alerts for potential compliance issues or unusual compliance-related patterns.

Alert management requires careful consideration of notification channels and escalation procedures. Systems should provide appropriate notification mechanisms, ensuring that alerts reach the right team members through effective communication channels. This includes configuring notification priorities, establishing escalation paths, and maintaining proper alert documentation.

The effectiveness of monitoring systems depends heavily on proper alert tuning. Teams should regularly review alert thresholds, update monitoring rules, and refine notification criteria to maintain an appropriate balance between security awareness and alert fatigue. This includes regular validation of alert effectiveness, updates to monitoring rules, and refinement of notification processes.

Integration with incident response procedures forms a crucial aspect of monitoring systems. Teams should maintain clear procedures for investigating alerts, establishing proper response protocols, and ensuring effective coordination during security incidents. This includes proper documentation of response procedures, regular testing of response capabilities, and maintenance of response team readiness.

The success of monitoring and alerting systems relies on consistent maintenance and regular updates. Teams should periodically review monitoring effectiveness, update alert criteria based on new threats, and ensure all team members maintain proper understanding of monitoring procedures. Regular refinement of monitoring practices helps maintain robust security awareness throughout contract operations.

50. DeFi Security Patterns

DeFi security patterns represent a specialized set of security considerations unique to decentralized finance applications. As DeFi protocols manage significant financial value and interact with complex financial instruments, implementing robust security patterns becomes crucial for protecting user assets and maintaining protocol integrity.

Composability security forms a fundamental aspect of DeFi protocol design. As DeFi applications frequently interact with multiple protocols and rely on external contracts, implementing secure composability patterns becomes essential. This includes careful validation of external contract interactions, implementing proper checks for return values, and maintaining awareness of potential interaction risks. Protocols should implement circuit breakers and interaction limits to protect against cascading failures in connected systems.

Liquidity pool security requires specialized attention in DeFi applications. Protocols must implement robust mechanisms to prevent manipulation of pool balances, protect against flash loan attacks, and maintain proper price discovery mechanisms. This includes implementing proper slippage controls, maintaining balance ratio limits, and implementing circuit breakers for unusual trading activity. Advanced mathematical models should validate pool operations and detect potential manipulation attempts.

Price oracle security represents a critical concern in DeFi protocols. Applications must implement robust oracle usage patterns, protecting against price manipulation and ensuring reliable price data. This includes using time-weighted average prices, implementing multiple oracle sources, and maintaining proper validation of price feeds. Protocols should implement circuit breakers for unusual price movements and maintain proper bounds checking on oracle data.

Yield farming security requires careful consideration of reward distribution mechanisms. Protocols must implement secure reward calculation systems, protect against manipulation of farming strategies, and maintain proper distribution controls. This includes implementing proper vesting schedules, maintaining accurate reward tracking, and protecting against exploitation of reward mechanisms. Systems should implement proper validation of farming activities and maintain appropriate limits on reward claims.

Lending protocol security focuses on maintaining proper collateralization and liquidation mechanisms. Applications must implement secure lending patterns, protect against manipulation of collateral values, and maintain proper liquidation procedures. This includes implementing proper collateral ratio calculations, maintaining secure liquidation triggers, and protecting against flash loan exploitation. Protocols should implement proper validation of lending operations and maintain appropriate safety margins.

Token integration security requires careful consideration of token interaction patterns. Protocols must implement secure token handling mechanisms, protect against malicious token contracts, and maintain proper balance tracking. This includes implementing proper token validation, maintaining secure transfer mechanisms, and protecting against token manipulation attacks. Systems should implement proper checks for token behavior and maintain appropriate integration controls.

Governance security represents a crucial aspect of DeFi protocol design. Applications must implement secure voting mechanisms, protect against manipulation of governance processes, and maintain proper proposal execution controls. This includes implementing proper voting power calculations, maintaining secure proposal queues, and protecting against governance attacks. Protocols should implement proper validation of governance activities and maintain appropriate timelock mechanisms.

Fee management security requires careful implementation of fee collection and distribution mechanisms. Protocols must implement secure fee calculation systems, protect against fee manipulation, and maintain proper distribution controls. This includes implementing proper fee tracking, maintaining secure fee collection mechanisms, and protecting against fee exploitation. Systems should implement proper validation of fee operations and maintain appropriate distribution controls.

Flash loan security represents a specialized concern in DeFi protocols. Applications must implement secure flash loan mechanisms, protect against exploitation of atomic transactions, and maintain proper validation of loan operations. This includes implementing proper loan validation, maintaining secure repayment checks, and protecting against complex attack vectors. Protocols should implement proper bounds on flash loan amounts and maintain appropriate usage controls.

Staking security requires careful implementation of stake management mechanisms. Protocols must implement secure staking systems, protect against stake manipulation, and maintain proper reward distribution. This includes implementing proper stake tracking, maintaining secure unstaking procedures, and protecting against staking exploits. Systems should implement proper validation of staking operations and maintain appropriate lockup controls.

Emergency response patterns form a crucial aspect of DeFi security. Protocols must implement proper emergency procedures, maintain effective circuit breakers, and ensure proper governance control during emergencies. This includes implementing proper pause mechanisms, maintaining secure upgrade paths, and protecting user assets during emergencies. Systems should implement proper emergency controls and maintain appropriate response procedures.

Economic security patterns help protect against manipulation of protocol economics. Applications must implement proper economic controls, protect against market manipulation, and maintain proper balance of incentives. This includes implementing proper pricing mechanisms, maintaining secure market operations, and protecting against economic attacks. Protocols should implement proper validation of economic activities and maintain appropriate market controls.

Integration security patterns help protect against risks from protocol integrations. Applications must implement proper integration controls, protect against malicious integrations, and maintain proper validation of external interactions. This includes implementing proper integration checks, maintaining secure interaction patterns, and protecting against integration exploits. Systems should implement proper validation of integrated components and maintain appropriate security controls.

Testing patterns for DeFi protocols require specialized consideration of financial scenarios. Applications must implement comprehensive testing frameworks, maintain proper coverage of financial operations, and ensure thorough validation of protocol behavior. This includes implementing proper economic simulations, maintaining secure test environments, and protecting against test manipulation. Protocols should implement proper validation of test scenarios and maintain appropriate testing controls.

The success of DeFi security patterns relies on continuous monitoring and adaptation. Teams must regularly review security effectiveness, update protection mechanisms based on new threats, and maintain proper understanding of evolving attack vectors. Regular refinement of security patterns helps maintain robust protection throughout protocol operations.

51. NFT Security Considerations

NFT security represents a critical aspect of blockchain development, particularly as non-fungible tokens continue to gain prominence in digital asset ecosystems. Securing NFT smart contracts requires specific considerations beyond traditional token security patterns to protect unique digital assets and their associated metadata.

Access control mechanisms form the foundation of NFT security. Implementing robust permission systems ensures that only authorized parties can mint, transfer, or modify NFTs. Smart contracts should clearly define and enforce roles such as contract owners, approved operators, and marketplace interfaces. These permissions must be carefully managed to prevent unauthorized access while maintaining necessary functionality for legitimate operations.

Metadata security represents a crucial aspect of NFT implementation. The integrity and availability of NFT metadata must be protected through proper storage mechanisms and access controls. On-chain metadata should be properly validated and protected against manipulation, while off-chain metadata requires secure storage solutions and reliable access mechanisms. Implementing proper URI validation and maintaining secure links between tokens and their metadata helps preserve NFT value and authenticity.

Minting security requires careful consideration to prevent abuse and maintain token scarcity. Smart contracts should implement proper controls over minting processes, including maximum supply limits, rate limiting, and proper validation of minting conditions. This includes implementing secure payment handling for paid mints, maintaining proper tracking of minted tokens, and protecting against exploitation of minting mechanisms. Systems should validate minting requests and maintain appropriate controls over token creation.

Transfer security patterns protect NFT ownership and prevent unauthorized movement of tokens. Implementing proper transfer validation ensures that only authorized parties can initiate transfers and that tokens move according to defined rules. This includes proper implementation of transfer functions, maintaining accurate ownership records, and protecting against transfer exploitation. Smart contracts should validate transfer requests and maintain appropriate controls over token movement.

Marketplace integration security focuses on safe interaction with NFT trading platforms. Smart contracts must implement secure listing mechanisms, protect against manipulation of sale processes, and maintain proper royalty distribution. This includes implementing secure price validation, maintaining proper escrow mechanisms, and protecting against marketplace exploitation. Systems should validate trading operations and maintain appropriate controls over marketplace interactions.

Royalty implementation security ensures proper distribution of secondary sale proceeds. Smart contracts must implement secure royalty calculation mechanisms, protect against manipulation of royalty payments, and maintain proper distribution controls. This includes implementing accurate royalty tracking, maintaining secure payment mechanisms, and protecting against royalty evasion. Protocols should validate royalty calculations and maintain appropriate distribution controls.

Batch operation security becomes particularly important for NFT collections. Smart contracts must implement secure mechanisms for handling multiple tokens simultaneously, protect against exploitation of batch operations, and maintain proper validation of bulk transactions. This includes implementing proper iteration controls, maintaining secure state updates, and protecting against batch operation attacks. Systems should validate batch requests and maintain appropriate limits on bulk operations.

Storage optimization patterns help manage the costs associated with NFT data. Smart contracts must implement efficient storage mechanisms, protect against excessive gas costs, and maintain proper data accessibility. This includes implementing proper data structures, maintaining efficient metadata access, and protecting against storage exploitation. Protocols should optimize storage operations while maintaining appropriate security controls.

Upgradeability patterns for NFT contracts require careful consideration. Implementing secure upgrade mechanisms ensures that contracts can be improved while protecting existing tokens and their properties. This includes implementing proper upgrade controls, maintaining token persistence, and protecting against upgrade exploitation. Systems should validate upgrade operations and maintain appropriate controls over contract evolution.

Random number generation security becomes crucial for NFT applications involving randomized attributes or distributions. Smart contracts must implement secure randomness mechanisms, protect against manipulation of random processes, and maintain proper entropy sources. This includes implementing proper seed generation, maintaining secure random number derivation, and protecting against randomness exploitation. Protocols should validate random operations and maintain appropriate controls over randomized processes.

Time-based security patterns protect against manipulation of temporal aspects in NFT systems. Smart contracts must implement secure timing mechanisms, protect against timestamp manipulation, and maintain proper temporal validation. This includes implementing proper time checks, maintaining secure scheduling mechanisms, and protecting against timing attacks. Systems should validate temporal operations and maintain appropriate controls over time-based functions.

Cross-chain NFT security requires specialized consideration as tokens move between different blockchain networks. Smart contracts must implement secure bridge mechanisms, protect against cross-chain exploitation, and maintain proper validation of token transfers. This includes implementing proper bridge controls, maintaining secure cross-chain state, and protecting against bridge attacks. Protocols should validate cross-chain operations and maintain appropriate controls over token bridging.

Gas efficiency patterns become particularly important for NFT operations involving multiple tokens. Smart contracts must implement efficient processing mechanisms, protect against excessive gas costs, and maintain proper operation completion. This includes implementing proper batch processing, maintaining efficient state updates, and protecting against gas-based attacks. Systems should optimize gas usage while maintaining appropriate security controls.

Testing patterns for NFT contracts require comprehensive coverage of token operations. Smart contracts must implement thorough testing frameworks, maintain proper validation of token functionality, and ensure complete coverage of security mechanisms. This includes implementing proper test scenarios, maintaining secure test environments, and protecting against test manipulation. Protocols should validate test coverage and maintain appropriate testing controls.

The effectiveness of NFT security patterns relies on continuous monitoring and adaptation. Teams must regularly review security measures, update protection mechanisms based on new threats, and maintain awareness of evolving attack vectors. Regular assessment and refinement of security patterns helps ensure robust protection of NFT assets and operations throughout their lifecycle.

52. DAO Security Implementation

Decentralized Autonomous Organizations (DAOs) represent complex governance systems that require robust security implementations to protect both assets and voting mechanisms. The implementation of secure DAO structures demands careful consideration of multiple security layers, from access control to vote counting integrity.

Governance token security forms the foundation of DAO implementation. Smart contracts must implement secure token distribution mechanisms that fairly allocate voting power while preventing manipulation. This includes careful implementation of token transfer restrictions, vesting schedules, and delegation mechanisms. The contract should maintain accurate token balances and voting power calculations while protecting against attempts to concentrate control through token accumulation or flash loan attacks.

Proposal mechanisms require particularly robust security measures. Smart contracts must implement secure proposal creation and validation systems that prevent spam while ensuring legitimate proposals can be submitted. This includes implementing proper threshold requirements, maintaining accurate proposal queues, and protecting against proposal flooding attacks. The system should validate proposal parameters and enforce appropriate cooling periods between submissions to prevent system abuse.

Voting security represents a critical aspect of DAO implementation. Smart contracts must protect the integrity of voting processes through secure vote counting mechanisms, protection against double voting, and maintenance of vote privacy when required. Implementation should include proper vote weight calculation, timestamp validation, and protection against last-minute vote manipulation. The system must maintain accurate vote tallies while preventing various forms of vote buying or delegation attacks.

Timelock mechanisms provide essential security for DAO operations. Smart contracts should implement secure delay periods between proposal approval and execution to allow stakeholders time to react to potentially malicious proposals. This includes proper implementation of timelock controls, maintenance of execution queues, and protection against timestamp manipulation. The system should enforce appropriate waiting periods while maintaining flexibility for emergency actions when necessary.

Treasury management security becomes paramount as DAOs often control significant assets. Smart contracts must implement secure multi-signature requirements for treasury operations, maintain proper access controls, and protect against unauthorized withdrawals. This includes implementing proper spending limits, maintaining accurate accounting, and protecting against various forms of treasury drainage attacks. The system should validate all treasury operations while maintaining appropriate controls over fund movement.

Delegation patterns require careful security consideration. Smart contracts must implement secure delegation mechanisms that accurately track voting power transfer while preventing abuse. This includes proper implementation of delegation chains, maintenance of delegation history, and protection against circular delegation attacks. The system should validate delegation operations and maintain appropriate controls over voting power transfer.

Emergency response mechanisms must be properly secured in DAO implementations. Smart contracts should include properly controlled pause functions, secure upgrade paths, and protected emergency actions. This includes implementing proper emergency controls, maintaining accurate state during emergencies, and protecting against exploitation of emergency mechanisms. The system should validate emergency operations while maintaining appropriate controls over exceptional circumstances.

Quorum requirements need secure implementation to prevent manipulation. Smart contracts must implement proper participation thresholds, maintain accurate counting mechanisms, and protect against artificial quorum manipulation. This includes implementing proper quorum calculation, maintaining accurate participation tracking, and protecting against last-minute voting attacks. The system should validate quorum achievements while maintaining appropriate controls over decision thresholds.

Execution security patterns protect the implementation of approved proposals. Smart contracts must implement secure execution mechanisms, maintain proper validation of execution conditions, and protect against malicious proposal execution. This includes implementing proper execution delays, maintaining accurate execution states, and protecting against various forms of execution attacks. The system should validate execution requests while maintaining appropriate controls over proposal implementation.

Integration security becomes crucial when DAOs interact with external protocols. Smart contracts must implement secure interface mechanisms, maintain proper validation of external calls, and protect against various forms of integration exploitation. This includes implementing proper interface controls, maintaining secure external state tracking, and protecting against malicious external contract interaction. The system should validate all external operations while maintaining appropriate security boundaries.

Incentive mechanism security ensures proper alignment of participant interests. Smart contracts must implement secure reward distribution, maintain proper incentive calculations, and protect against gaming of reward systems. This includes implementing proper reward tracking, maintaining accurate distribution mechanisms, and protecting against various forms of reward exploitation. The system should validate incentive operations while maintaining appropriate controls over reward distribution.

Upgrade patterns for DAO contracts require particular attention to security. Smart contracts must implement secure upgrade mechanisms that protect existing governance structures while allowing for necessary improvements. This includes implementing proper upgrade controls, maintaining governance continuity, and protecting against malicious upgrades. The system should validate upgrade operations while maintaining appropriate controls over contract evolution.

Testing frameworks for DAO implementations must be comprehensive. Smart contracts require thorough testing of governance mechanisms, vote counting accuracy, and security controls. This includes implementing proper test scenarios, maintaining secure test environments, and protecting against test manipulation. The system should validate test coverage while maintaining appropriate testing controls for all governance functions.

The effectiveness of DAO security patterns relies on continuous monitoring and adaptation. Teams must regularly review governance mechanisms, update security controls based on observed behavior, and maintain awareness of potential attack vectors. Regular assessment and refinement of security patterns helps ensure robust protection of DAO operations and assets throughout their lifecycle.

53. Layer 2 Security Considerations

Layer 2 scaling solutions have introduced new security considerations that smart contract developers must carefully address when building applications that operate across multiple layers of blockchain infrastructure. Understanding and implementing proper security measures for Layer 2 interactions is crucial for maintaining the integrity and safety of decentralized applications.

State transition verification represents one of the most critical security aspects of Layer 2 implementations. Smart contracts must implement robust verification mechanisms to ensure that state transitions between Layer 1 and Layer 2 are accurate and tamper-proof. This includes proper validation of state roots, maintenance of merkle proofs, and protection against fraudulent state submissions. Developers must carefully implement challenge periods and dispute resolution mechanisms to prevent malicious actors from submitting incorrect state transitions.

Bridge security becomes paramount when implementing Layer 2 solutions. Smart contracts handling asset transfers between layers must implement secure locking and unlocking mechanisms, maintain accurate accounting of bridged assets, and protect against various bridge exploitation attempts. This includes proper implementation of withdrawal delays, maintenance of bridge limits, and protection against replay attacks. Bridge contracts should implement robust validation mechanisms for cross-layer messages and maintain appropriate security controls over asset movement.

Rollup security patterns require particular attention in Layer 2 implementations. Smart contracts must properly handle transaction batching, maintain secure compression mechanisms, and protect against various forms of rollup manipulation. This includes implementing proper batch validation, maintaining accurate transaction ordering, and protecting against malicious operator behavior. The system should validate batch submissions while maintaining appropriate controls over transaction processing.

Data availability considerations introduce unique security challenges in Layer 2 systems. Smart contracts must implement proper data availability verification, maintain accurate data roots, and protect against data withholding attacks. This includes implementing proper data posting requirements, maintaining secure data availability proofs, and protecting against various forms of data manipulation. The system should validate data availability while maintaining appropriate controls over data access.

Operator security becomes crucial in Layer 2 implementations. Smart contracts must implement proper operator validation mechanisms, maintain accurate operator registries, and protect against malicious operator actions. This includes implementing proper operator rotation, maintaining secure operator stakes, and protecting against various forms of operator collusion. The system should validate operator actions while maintaining appropriate controls over operator privileges.

Exit mechanism security ensures users can safely withdraw assets from Layer 2 systems. Smart contracts must implement secure withdrawal processes, maintain proper challenge periods, and protect against fraudulent exit attempts. This includes implementing proper exit verification, maintaining accurate exit queues, and protecting against various forms of exit fraud. The system should validate withdrawal requests while maintaining appropriate controls over asset exits.

Sequencer security patterns protect the ordering of Layer 2 transactions. Smart contracts must implement proper sequencing mechanisms, maintain accurate transaction ordering, and protect against front-running at the sequencer level. This includes implementing proper sequencing rules, maintaining secure ordering proofs, and protecting against sequencer manipulation. The system should validate transaction sequences while maintaining appropriate controls over transaction ordering.

Force transaction mechanisms require careful security implementation. Smart contracts must implement secure forced transaction submission, maintain proper validation of forced transactions, and protect against abuse of force mechanisms. This includes implementing proper force transaction delays, maintaining accurate forced transaction queues, and protecting against various forms of forced transaction exploitation.

State synchronization security ensures consistency between layers. Smart contracts must implement proper synchronization mechanisms, maintain accurate state roots, and protect against state divergence. This includes implementing proper state verification, maintaining secure state updates, and protecting against various forms of state manipulation. The system should validate state synchronization while maintaining appropriate controls over state consistency.

Gas token handling introduces specific security considerations in Layer 2 systems. Smart contracts must implement secure gas pricing mechanisms, maintain proper gas markets, and protect against gas price manipulation. This includes implementing proper gas limits, maintaining accurate gas accounting, and protecting against various forms of gas exploitation. The system should validate gas operations while maintaining appropriate controls over gas usage.

Upgrade patterns for Layer 2 contracts require particular attention to security. Smart contracts must implement secure upgrade mechanisms that maintain system stability while allowing for necessary improvements. This includes implementing proper upgrade delays, maintaining system continuity, and protecting against malicious upgrades. The system should validate upgrade operations while maintaining appropriate controls over contract evolution.

Monitoring systems become essential for Layer 2 security. Smart contracts must implement proper event logging, maintain accurate monitoring hooks, and protect against monitoring circumvention. This includes implementing proper alerting mechanisms, maintaining secure monitoring infrastructure, and protecting against various forms of monitoring evasion. The system should validate monitoring data while maintaining appropriate controls over system observation.

Integration security with Layer 1 requires careful consideration. Smart contracts must implement secure communication channels, maintain proper message validation, and protect against cross-layer attacks. This includes implementing proper message passing, maintaining secure cross-layer state, and protecting against various forms of cross-layer exploitation. The system should validate all cross-layer operations while maintaining appropriate security boundaries between layers.

The effectiveness of Layer 2 security patterns relies on comprehensive testing and continuous monitoring. Teams must regularly review security mechanisms, update controls based on observed behavior, and maintain awareness of potential attack vectors across both layers. Regular assessment and refinement of security patterns helps ensure robust protection of Layer 2 operations throughout their lifecycle.

54. Cross-Chain Security

Cross-chain security has emerged as a critical consideration in the blockchain ecosystem as more decentralized applications operate across multiple chains and leverage various bridging mechanisms. The interconnected nature of cross-chain operations introduces unique security challenges that developers must carefully address to protect user assets and maintain system integrity.

Message verification represents the foundation of secure cross-chain communication. Smart contracts must implement robust verification mechanisms for messages passed between chains, ensuring authenticity and preventing manipulation. This includes proper validation of message origins, verification of chain identifiers, and protection against replay attacks. Developers should implement nonce-based systems to prevent message reuse and maintain strict validation of cross-chain message formats.

Asset bridging security requires particular attention when implementing cross-chain functionality. Smart contracts handling asset transfers between chains must implement secure locking mechanisms, maintain accurate accounting of bridged assets, and protect against various bridge exploitation attempts. This includes implementing appropriate time delays for large transfers, maintaining bridge transfer limits, and ensuring proper collateralization of bridged assets. Bridge contracts should implement multiple validation layers and maintain strict controls over asset movement between chains.

Consensus verification becomes crucial in cross-chain operations. Smart contracts must properly validate the consensus mechanisms of partner chains, implement secure verification of block finality, and protect against various consensus manipulation attempts. This includes maintaining accurate records of validator sets, implementing proper finality thresholds, and protecting against chain reorganization attacks.

The system should maintain appropriate waiting periods based on the security characteristics of different chains.

Atomic operations across chains present unique security challenges. Smart contracts must implement secure mechanisms for ensuring atomicity of cross-chain transactions, maintain proper rollback capabilities, and protect against partial execution attacks. This includes implementing proper timeout mechanisms, maintaining accurate transaction states across chains, and protecting against various forms of transaction manipulation. The system should maintain appropriate safeguards for handling failed cross-chain operations.

Chain identification security ensures proper routing and validation of cross-chain messages. Smart contracts must implement secure chain identification mechanisms, maintain accurate chain registries, and protect against chain spoofing attempts. This includes implementing proper chain verification, maintaining secure chain identifiers, and protecting against various forms of chain impersonation. The system should validate chain identities while maintaining appropriate controls over cross-chain routing.

Relayer security becomes essential in cross-chain systems. Smart contracts must implement proper relayer validation mechanisms, maintain accurate relayer registries, and protect against malicious relayer behavior. This includes implementing proper relayer rotation, maintaining secure relayer stakes, and protecting against various forms of relayer collusion. The system should validate relayer actions while maintaining appropriate controls over message propagation.

Fee handling across chains requires careful security implementation. Smart contracts must implement secure fee collection mechanisms, maintain proper fee markets, and protect against fee manipulation across chains. This includes implementing proper fee estimation, maintaining accurate fee accounting, and protecting against various forms of fee exploitation. The system should validate fee payments while maintaining appropriate controls over cross-chain cost structures.

State synchronization between chains demands robust security measures. Smart contracts must implement proper state verification mechanisms, maintain accurate state proofs, and protect against state manipulation across chains. This includes implementing proper state validation, maintaining secure state updates, and protecting against various forms of state divergence. The system should maintain appropriate controls over cross-chain state consistency.

Emergency response mechanisms become crucial in cross-chain systems. Smart contracts must implement secure emergency stops, maintain proper circuit breakers, and protect against cascading failures across chains. This includes implementing proper pause mechanisms, maintaining secure recovery procedures, and protecting against various forms of system-wide exploitation. The system should maintain appropriate controls for handling cross-chain emergencies.

Upgrade coordination across chains requires particular attention to security. Smart contracts must implement secure upgrade mechanisms that maintain system consistency across all participating chains. This includes implementing proper upgrade synchronization, maintaining system continuity, and protecting against incompatible upgrades. The system should validate upgrade operations while maintaining appropriate controls over cross-chain contract evolution.

Monitoring and alerting systems must account for cross-chain operations. Smart contracts must implement proper event logging across chains, maintain accurate monitoring hooks, and protect against monitoring blind spots. This includes implementing proper cross-chain alerting mechanisms, maintaining secure monitoring infrastructure, and protecting against various forms of monitoring evasion. The system should validate monitoring data while maintaining appropriate visibility across all participating chains.

Asset representation across chains demands careful security consideration. Smart contracts must implement secure asset wrapping mechanisms, maintain proper asset backing, and protect against various forms of asset manipulation. This includes implementing proper asset verification, maintaining accurate asset registries, and protecting against unauthorized asset creation. The system should maintain appropriate controls over cross-chain asset representation.

The implementation of cross-chain security patterns requires comprehensive testing across all participating chains. Teams must regularly review security mechanisms, update controls based on observed behavior, and maintain awareness of potential attack vectors across the entire system. Regular security assessments and refinement of cross-chain security patterns helps ensure robust protection of cross-chain operations throughout their lifecycle.

55. Privacy Patterns

Privacy patterns in smart contract development represent a critical aspect of blockchain applications, particularly as concerns around data protection and confidentiality continue to grow. While public blockchains inherently make all transaction data visible, various techniques and patterns can be employed to enhance privacy while maintaining the benefits of decentralized systems.

Zero knowledge proofs have emerged as a fundamental building block for privacy-preserving smart contracts. These cryptographic constructs allow one party to prove to another that a statement is true without revealing any information beyond the validity of the statement itself. In smart contracts, ZK proofs can be implemented to validate transactions, verify identities, or confirm compliance with certain conditions while keeping the underlying data private. Developers must carefully implement ZK proof verification, maintain proper setup parameters, and ensure the security of proof generation and validation processes.

Commitment schemes provide another essential privacy pattern in smart contract development. By allowing users to commit to a value without revealing it immediately, these schemes enable various privacy-preserving protocols. Smart contracts can implement hash-based commitments, maintain proper reveal mechanisms, and protect against premature value disclosure. This pattern proves particularly useful in applications requiring sealed bids, private voting systems, or time-locked revelations.

Ring signatures offer privacy enhancement by allowing a user to sign a message on behalf of a group without revealing which group member actually created the signature. Smart contracts can implement ring signature verification, maintain proper ring member sets, and protect against signature linking attempts. This pattern proves valuable in applications requiring anonymous but verifiable actions, such as private voting systems or anonymous donations.

Stealth addresses provide transaction privacy by generating one-time addresses for each transaction, preventing address reuse and making it difficult to link multiple transactions to the same entity. Smart contracts can implement stealth address generation, maintain proper key management, and protect against address correlation attempts. This pattern proves particularly useful in applications requiring payment privacy or anonymous asset transfers.

State channels represent another privacy pattern by moving transactions off-chain while maintaining security guarantees. By conducting multiple transactions privately between parties and only settling the final state on-chain, state channels can significantly enhance transaction privacy. Smart contracts must implement secure channel opening and closing mechanisms, maintain proper state updates, and protect against various forms of channel manipulation.

Encrypted storage patterns allow smart contracts to handle encrypted data while maintaining functionality. By implementing proper encryption schemes, managing key access, and protecting against unauthorized decryption, contracts can process sensitive information without exposing it publicly. This pattern proves valuable in applications requiring confidential data storage or private information processing.

Mixer protocols enhance transaction privacy by breaking the link between source and destination addresses. Smart contracts can implement secure mixing mechanisms, maintain proper anonymity sets, and protect against various deanonymization attempts. This pattern proves particularly useful in applications requiring strong transaction privacy or fungible token transfers.

Private token standards implement privacy-preserving features at the token level. Smart contracts can implement confidential token transfers, maintain proper balance privacy, and protect against various forms of transaction analysis. This includes implementing proper encryption schemes, maintaining secure viewing keys, and protecting against balance tracking attempts.

Proxy re-encryption patterns allow secure sharing of encrypted data between parties without exposing the underlying information. Smart contracts can implement secure re-encryption mechanisms, maintain proper key management, and protect against unauthorized access attempts. This pattern proves valuable in applications requiring controlled data sharing or selective disclosure.

Verifiable delay functions provide privacy through time-locked revelations. Smart contracts can implement secure delay mechanisms, maintain proper time constraints, and protect against premature information disclosure. This pattern proves particularly useful in applications requiring committed information release or time-based privacy.

Access control privacy patterns implement fine-grained permissions while maintaining confidentiality. Smart contracts can implement role-based privacy, maintain proper permission structures, and protect against unauthorized information access. This includes implementing proper encryption schemes, maintaining secure access controls, and protecting against permission inference attacks.

Query privacy patterns protect against information leakage through smart contract interactions. By implementing proper query obfuscation, maintaining secure lookup mechanisms, and protecting against various forms of query analysis, contracts can prevent unauthorized information gathering through interaction patterns.

Event privacy patterns ensure that contract events don't leak sensitive information. Smart contracts must implement secure event emission, maintain proper information filtering, and protect against various forms of event analysis. This includes implementing proper encryption schemes, maintaining secure event structures, and protecting against event correlation attempts.

The implementation of privacy patterns requires careful consideration of the tradeoffs between privacy, functionality, and cost. Gas consumption often increases with privacy-enhancing features, and developers must balance these concerns against application requirements. Regular security assessments and privacy audits help ensure that implemented patterns maintain their effectiveness throughout the contract lifecycle.

Successful privacy pattern implementation requires comprehensive testing and validation. Teams must regularly review privacy mechanisms, update controls based on new attack vectors, and maintain awareness of evolving privacy technologies. The continuous refinement of privacy patterns helps ensure robust protection of sensitive information while maintaining smart contract functionality.

56. Gas Token Implementation

Gas tokens represent a unique innovation in smart contract development that allows developers to tokenize and trade gas costs on the Ethereum network. This chapter explores the implementation details, security considerations, and best practices for creating and managing gas tokens effectively.

The fundamental concept behind gas tokens revolves around the storage refund mechanism in Ethereum. When storage slots are cleared (set to zero), the EVM provides a gas refund. Gas tokens exploit this mechanism by storing data when gas prices are low and clearing it when gas prices are high, effectively allowing users to arbitrage gas prices over time.

A basic gas token implementation starts with a storage mapping that can hold arbitrary data. The contract should include functions for minting tokens (storing data) and burning tokens (clearing storage). The minting process involves writing data to storage slots during periods of low gas prices. This operation is relatively expensive but becomes valuable when gas prices rise. The burning process clears these storage slots, triggering the gas refund mechanism and potentially reducing the overall transaction cost.

Implementation of gas tokens requires careful consideration of storage patterns. Rather than using a simple boolean mapping, more sophisticated implementations might use bit packing techniques to maximize storage efficiency. Each storage slot can store multiple token units, reducing the overall storage overhead and improving gas efficiency during minting and burning operations.

The mint function in a gas token contract typically accepts a parameter specifying the number of tokens to create. The function must implement proper checks to prevent overflow conditions and ensure adequate gas is available for the operation. It should also include mechanisms to prevent excessive minting that could destabilize the system or create unusable token configurations.

Burning mechanisms must be implemented with particular attention to security. The burn function should verify ownership of tokens, implement proper access controls, and ensure that storage clearing operations execute correctly. Additionally, the contract should maintain accurate accounting of burned tokens to prevent double spending or invalid refund claims.

Gas token contracts must implement proper token transfer functionality. This includes standard ERC20 interface methods for allowance, transfer, and approval operations. However, gas token implementations often require additional safety checks to prevent manipulation of the storage refund mechanism during transfers.

Advanced gas token implementations might include batch operations for more efficient minting and burning. These operations allow users to mint or burn multiple tokens in a single transaction, potentially reducing the overall gas cost. However, batch operations must implement proper gas limits and security checks to prevent denial of service attacks.

Price oracle integration can enhance gas token functionality by automating minting and burning decisions based on current gas prices. The contract can implement interfaces to reliable gas price oracles, establish appropriate thresholds for automated operations, and maintain proper security controls around oracle data usage.

Storage slot management represents a critical aspect of gas token implementation. The contract must maintain proper tracking of used and available storage slots, implement efficient allocation mechanisms, and prevent fragmentation of storage space. This includes implementing proper cleanup mechanisms for abandoned or expired tokens.

Gas token contracts should implement emergency stop mechanisms to protect against potential vulnerabilities or unexpected behavior. This includes functions to pause minting and burning operations, mechanisms to recover from error states, and proper access controls for administrative functions.

Version management becomes particularly important for gas token implementations as network conditions and gas refund mechanics may change over time. The contract should include proper upgrade paths, maintain compatibility with existing token holdings, and implement secure migration mechanisms for future modifications.

Monitoring systems play a crucial role in gas token operation. The contract should emit appropriate events for all significant operations, maintain proper logging of storage state changes, and implement alerts for unusual activity patterns. This includes tracking minting and burning volumes, monitoring storage utilization, and analyzing gas price correlations.

Gas token economics require careful consideration during implementation. The contract should implement mechanisms to prevent market manipulation, maintain proper incentive structures, and ensure sustainable operation under varying network conditions. This includes implementing rate limiting mechanisms, establishing proper pricing models, and maintaining market stability controls.

Testing gas token implementations presents unique challenges due to the interaction with network gas mechanics. Comprehensive test suites should include simulation of various gas price scenarios, validation of refund mechanics, and verification of economic model assumptions. This includes implementing proper gas measurement tools, maintaining accurate test environments, and validating behavior under stress conditions.

Documentation for gas token implementations must be particularly detailed due to the complex interaction with network mechanics. This includes proper specification of minting and burning processes, clear explanation of economic models, and comprehensive guides for integration and usage. The documentation should also include proper security considerations and risk assessments.

Audit preparation for gas token contracts requires special attention to gas mechanics and economic models. This includes preparing proper specification documents, implementing comprehensive test coverage, and maintaining clear documentation of design decisions. The audit process should specifically address potential manipulation vectors, storage management efficiency, and economic model stability.

Future considerations for gas token implementations include potential changes to network gas mechanics, evolution of storage refund systems, and development of new optimization techniques. Contracts should maintain flexibility for future adaptations while ensuring secure operation under current conditions.

The successful implementation of gas tokens requires careful balance between technical efficiency, economic sustainability, and security considerations. Regular review and updates ensure that the implementation remains effective and secure as network conditions evolve. Proper attention to these aspects helps create robust and valuable gas token systems that provide genuine utility to the Ethereum ecosystem.

57. Contract Factory Patterns

Contract factory patterns represent a fundamental design approach in smart contract development that enables the automated creation and deployment of new contract instances. This chapter explores the implementation strategies, security considerations, and best practices for building robust contract factories in Solidity.

A contract factory is essentially a smart contract that creates other smart contracts. This pattern proves invaluable when applications need to deploy multiple instances of similar contracts, such as individual token contracts, user wallets, or game instances. The factory pattern provides a centralized and controlled way to manage contract creation while ensuring consistency and reducing deployment costs.

The basic implementation of a contract factory involves a main contract that contains the creation logic and maintains records of deployed contracts. The factory typically includes a creation function that accepts necessary parameters, deploys a new contract instance, and emits events to track the deployment. This pattern allows for standardized initialization, proper record keeping, and simplified contract management.

Memory management becomes crucial when implementing contract factories. The creation process must efficiently handle constructor parameters, properly initialize storage variables, and manage memory allocation during deployment. Developers must carefully consider the balance between storing deployment data on chain versus emitting events to maintain deployment records.

Security considerations for contract factories extend beyond typical smart contract vulnerabilities. The factory must implement proper access controls to prevent unauthorized contract creation, validate initialization parameters, and ensure proper initialization of deployed contracts. Additionally, the factory should maintain proper separation between contract instances to prevent cross contract interference.

Implementation of deterministic addresses for deployed contracts represents an advanced feature of contract factory patterns. By using CREATE2 opcode, factories can predict contract addresses before deployment, enabling more complex initialization patterns and improved integration with external systems. However, proper implementation requires careful consideration of salt values and initialization parameters.

Upgradeability patterns often integrate with contract factories to enable systematic updates across deployed instances. The factory can implement proxy patterns, maintain version controls, and manage upgrade processes for deployed contracts. This includes proper implementation of initialization functions, secure storage of implementation addresses, and careful management of upgrade permissions.

Gas optimization becomes particularly important in factory implementations due to the deployment costs associated with contract creation. The factory should implement efficient creation patterns, minimize storage usage, and optimize initialization processes. This includes proper use of assembly for deployment, efficient parameter encoding, and careful management of deployment overhead.

Event logging plays a crucial role in contract factories for maintaining deployment records and enabling external systems to track contract creation. The factory should emit detailed events for all deployments, including relevant parameters, addresses, and initialization data. This enables proper monitoring, simplifies integration, and maintains accurate deployment histories.

Template management represents another important aspect of contract factory implementation. The factory might maintain multiple contract templates, implement version control mechanisms, and manage template updates. This includes proper storage of bytecode, secure update mechanisms, and careful validation of template integrity.

Batch deployment capabilities can enhance factory functionality by enabling multiple contract deployments in single transactions. The implementation must carefully manage gas limits, implement proper failure handling, and maintain accurate deployment records. This includes proper parameter validation, efficient execution patterns, and secure state management.

Integration with external systems requires careful consideration in factory implementations. The factory should implement proper interfaces for external interaction, maintain accurate state synchronization, and provide necessary validation mechanisms. This includes implementing callback patterns, managing asynchronous operations, and maintaining proper security boundaries.

Testing factory implementations presents unique challenges due to the dynamic nature of contract creation. Test suites must verify deployment patterns, validate initialization processes, and ensure proper operation of created contracts. This includes implementing proper deployment verification, maintaining comprehensive test coverage, and validating complex interaction patterns.

Documentation for factory implementations must clearly specify creation patterns, initialization requirements, and integration guidelines. This includes proper documentation of parameter requirements, clear explanation of deployment processes, and comprehensive guides for factory usage. The documentation should also address security considerations and potential risks.

Factory economics require careful consideration during implementation. The factory should implement proper fee structures, maintain sustainable operation patterns, and ensure efficient resource utilization. This includes implementing proper payment mechanisms, managing deployment costs, and maintaining economic viability.

Monitoring systems become particularly important for factory operations. The factory should implement proper monitoring interfaces, maintain accurate deployment records, and enable efficient tracking of created contracts. This includes implementing proper alerting mechanisms, maintaining accurate statistics, and enabling effective operational oversight.

Future considerations for factory implementations include potential changes to contract creation mechanics, evolution of deployment patterns, and development of new optimization techniques. The implementation should maintain flexibility for future adaptations while ensuring secure operation under current conditions.

The successful implementation of contract factories requires careful attention to security, efficiency, and maintainability. Regular review and updates ensure that the factory remains effective and secure as requirements evolve. Proper consideration of these aspects helps create robust and valuable factory systems that enhance the development and deployment of smart contract applications.

58. Secure Wallet Integration

Secure wallet integration represents a critical aspect of decentralized application development, requiring careful consideration of security patterns, user experience, and interaction protocols. This chapter explores comprehensive approaches to implementing secure wallet connections while maintaining robust security standards and user privacy.

The foundation of secure wallet integration begins with proper protocol implementation. Smart contracts must implement standardized interfaces that enable seamless interaction with various wallet types while maintaining security boundaries. This includes proper implementation of signature verification, transaction authorization, and state management protocols that ensure secure wallet interactions.

Authentication mechanisms form a crucial component of wallet integration. Contracts must implement robust signature verification systems, maintain proper nonce management, and ensure secure session handling. The implementation should include proper validation of signed messages, secure storage of authentication states, and careful management of user permissions throughout the interaction lifecycle.

Transaction security requires particular attention in wallet integration patterns. The implementation must ensure proper validation of transaction parameters, maintain secure execution flows, and implement robust error handling. This includes proper gas estimation, secure parameter encoding, and careful management of transaction states to prevent unauthorized operations or malicious interactions.

User experience considerations play a vital role in secure wallet integration. The implementation should provide clear interaction patterns, maintain proper error messaging, and ensure intuitive operation flows. This includes implementing proper transaction previews, maintaining clear status indicators, and providing comprehensive feedback throughout the interaction process.

State management becomes particularly important when implementing wallet interactions. The contract must maintain proper tracking of wallet states, implement secure update mechanisms, and ensure proper synchronization across different components. This includes implementing proper storage patterns, maintaining accurate state transitions, and ensuring consistent operation across different interaction scenarios.

Multi wallet support represents an important feature of modern implementations. The contract should accommodate different wallet types, implement proper interface adaptations, and maintain consistent security across various wallet implementations. This includes proper handling of different signature schemes, maintaining compatibility with various wallet standards, and ensuring secure operation across different platforms.

Recovery mechanisms must be carefully implemented to handle potential issues. The contract should implement proper fallback patterns, maintain secure recovery processes, and ensure proper handling of edge cases. This includes implementing proper timeout mechanisms, maintaining secure state recovery, and ensuring proper handling of interrupted operations.

Privacy considerations become increasingly important in wallet interactions. The implementation must ensure proper protection of user data, maintain secure communication channels, and implement proper access controls. This includes proper encryption of sensitive data, secure handling of personal information, and careful management of visibility patterns across different interaction scenarios.

Gas management requires careful attention in wallet integration. The implementation should optimize gas usage, implement proper estimation mechanisms, and ensure efficient operation patterns. This includes proper implementation of gas saving techniques, maintaining efficient execution flows, and ensuring proper handling of gas related constraints.

Event logging plays a crucial role in maintaining proper interaction records. The contract should emit detailed events for significant operations, maintain proper audit trails, and enable effective monitoring of wallet interactions. This includes proper logging of authentication events, maintaining detailed transaction records, and enabling effective tracking of interaction patterns.

Integration testing becomes particularly important for wallet implementations. The test suite must verify different interaction scenarios, validate security mechanisms, and ensure proper operation across various conditions. This includes implementing comprehensive test coverage, maintaining proper integration tests, and ensuring effective validation of security features.

Error handling patterns must be carefully implemented to maintain secure operation. The contract should implement proper failure modes, maintain secure error recovery, and ensure proper handling of exceptional conditions. This includes implementing proper revert mechanisms, maintaining secure state handling, and ensuring proper recovery from various error conditions.

Monitoring systems become crucial for maintaining operational security. The implementation should enable proper tracking of wallet interactions, maintain accurate usage statistics, and enable effective detection of potential issues. This includes implementing proper alerting mechanisms, maintaining accurate monitoring data, and enabling effective operational oversight.

Version management requires careful consideration in wallet integration. The implementation should maintain proper compatibility handling, implement secure upgrade patterns, and ensure smooth transition across different versions. This includes proper handling of breaking changes, maintaining backward compatibility where possible, and ensuring secure migration patterns.

Documentation plays a vital role in ensuring proper implementation and usage. The documentation should clearly specify integration requirements, detail security considerations, and provide comprehensive usage guidelines. This includes proper documentation of authentication flows, detailed explanation of security features, and clear guidance on proper implementation patterns.

Future considerations must be taken into account during implementation. The contract should maintain flexibility for future adaptations, implement extensible patterns, and ensure adaptability to evolving requirements. This includes consideration of potential protocol changes, evolution of wallet standards, and development of new security requirements.

The successful implementation of secure wallet integration requires careful attention to multiple aspects of security, usability, and maintainability. Regular review and updates ensure that the implementation remains effective and secure as requirements evolve. Proper consideration of these aspects helps create robust and valuable wallet integration systems that enhance the security and functionality of decentralized applications.

59. Security Incident Response

Security incident response in blockchain applications requires a systematic and well-planned approach to handle potential security breaches, vulnerabilities, and other critical incidents that may affect smart contract operations. This chapter explores comprehensive strategies for implementing effective incident response mechanisms and maintaining operational security during critical situations.

A robust security incident response plan begins with proper preparation and documentation. Organizations must establish clear protocols for identifying, classifying, and responding to different types of security incidents. This includes defining severity levels, establishing communication channels, and maintaining detailed response procedures that can be quickly activated when incidents occur.

Incident detection mechanisms form the foundation of effective response systems. Smart contracts should implement proper monitoring systems, maintain comprehensive logging mechanisms, and enable quick identification of potential security issues. This includes implementing proper alerting thresholds, maintaining detailed audit trails, and ensuring effective tracking of contract operations that might indicate security problems.

The initial response to a security incident is crucial for minimizing potential damage. Organizations must maintain ready to execute procedures for immediate response, including mechanisms for contract pause or shutdown, secure communication protocols, and rapid assessment procedures. This includes maintaining proper access to emergency controls, implementing secure communication channels, and ensuring quick activation of response teams.

Assessment procedures must be thorough and systematic during incident response. The team should quickly evaluate the scope of the incident, identify affected components, and determine potential impact on contract operations and user assets. This includes proper analysis of transaction patterns, detailed examination of contract states, and comprehensive evaluation of potential exploitation vectors.

Communication strategies play a vital role in incident response. Organizations must maintain clear communication protocols, ensure proper notification of stakeholders, and provide accurate updates throughout the incident lifecycle. This includes proper management of public communications, maintaining secure channels for technical updates, and ensuring effective coordination among response team members.

Containment strategies must be implemented quickly to prevent further damage. This includes activating emergency stops, implementing additional security controls, and ensuring proper isolation of affected components. The implementation should include proper circuit breaker patterns, secure state management during incidents, and effective mechanisms for limiting potential damage.

Evidence collection becomes crucial for both immediate response and future prevention. The team must maintain proper procedures for collecting and preserving relevant data, implementing secure logging mechanisms, and ensuring proper documentation of incident details. This includes proper collection of transaction data, secure storage of relevant logs, and comprehensive documentation of incident progression.

Recovery procedures must be carefully planned and executed. Organizations should maintain proper mechanisms for restoring normal operations, implementing necessary security updates, and ensuring proper validation of recovered states. This includes proper implementation of recovery protocols, secure deployment of fixes, and comprehensive testing of restored functionality.

Post incident analysis forms a crucial part of the response cycle. Teams must conduct thorough reviews of incident causes, implement necessary improvements, and update response procedures based on lessons learned. This includes proper analysis of exploitation vectors, detailed review of response effectiveness, and comprehensive updates to security measures.

User impact management requires careful attention during security incidents. Organizations must maintain proper procedures for handling user concerns, implementing compensation mechanisms where necessary, and ensuring clear communication about impact and resolution. This includes proper handling of affected transactions, secure management of user assets, and clear communication about resolution steps.

Technical debt assessment becomes important following security incidents. Teams must evaluate necessary updates to contract implementations, identify potential vulnerabilities in related systems, and plan comprehensive improvements to prevent similar incidents. This includes proper review of contract architecture, detailed analysis of security patterns, and comprehensive planning of necessary updates.

Documentation updates form a crucial part of incident response. Organizations must maintain detailed records of incidents, update security procedures based on experience, and ensure proper documentation of implemented changes. This includes maintaining comprehensive incident reports, updating response procedures, and ensuring proper documentation of security improvements.

Testing procedures must be updated to reflect learned lessons. Teams should implement additional security tests, enhance monitoring systems, and improve validation procedures based on incident experience. This includes implementing new test scenarios, enhancing security validation, and improving continuous monitoring systems.

Regulatory compliance must be considered during incident response. Organizations should ensure proper reporting to relevant authorities, maintain compliance with security requirements, and implement necessary updates to meet regulatory standards. This includes proper documentation of incident details, maintenance of required reports, and implementation of necessary compliance measures.

Long term improvements must be planned based on incident experience. Organizations should implement systematic updates to security measures, enhance monitoring capabilities, and improve response procedures based on practical experience. This includes proper evolution of security patterns, enhancement of detection mechanisms, and continuous improvement of response capabilities.

Training and preparation become increasingly important following incidents. Teams must maintain updated training programs, implement regular drills, and ensure proper preparation for potential future incidents. This includes regular security training, practical response exercises, and continuous improvement of team capabilities.

The implementation of effective security incident response requires careful attention to multiple aspects of preparation, execution, and improvement. Regular review and updates ensure that response capabilities remain effective as threats evolve. Proper consideration of these aspects helps create robust and effective incident response systems that enhance the security and reliability of blockchain applications.

60. Post-Deployment Monitoring

Post deployment monitoring represents a critical aspect of maintaining secure and efficient smart contract operations in production environments. Effective monitoring strategies help identify potential issues before they become critical problems and ensure the continued health of deployed contracts.

Comprehensive monitoring begins with establishing proper metrics and indicators that provide insight into contract operations. These include transaction volumes, gas usage patterns, function call frequencies, and state changes. By tracking these fundamental metrics, teams can establish baseline behavior patterns and quickly identify anomalies that might indicate security issues or operational problems.

Smart contracts should implement proper event emission patterns to facilitate effective monitoring. Events should be structured to provide meaningful insights into contract operations while maintaining efficient gas usage. This includes proper indexing of critical parameters, meaningful event structures, and efficient data encoding patterns that balance information content with gas costs.

Real time monitoring systems form an essential component of post deployment operations. These systems should track contract interactions, monitor state changes, and provide immediate alerts for unusual patterns. Implementation should include proper threshold management, efficient data processing, and effective alerting mechanisms that can quickly notify relevant team members of potential issues.

Historical analysis capabilities provide valuable insights into contract behavior patterns. Monitoring systems should maintain proper historical records, implement efficient data storage patterns, and provide comprehensive analysis tools. This enables teams to identify long term trends, recognize developing issues, and make informed decisions about contract maintenance and updates.

Gas usage patterns require particular attention in post deployment monitoring. Systems should track gas consumption across different functions, monitor changes in gas costs, and identify potential optimization opportunities. This includes proper analysis of transaction costs, monitoring of gas price impacts, and identification of potential gas optimization opportunities.

User interaction patterns provide valuable insights into contract usage and potential issues. Monitoring systems should track user behavior patterns, identify unusual activity, and maintain proper records of interaction frequencies. This helps identify potential security issues, understand user needs, and guide future contract improvements.

State consistency monitoring becomes crucial for complex contract systems. Teams should implement proper validation mechanisms, maintain state integrity checks, and ensure proper tracking of critical state variables. This includes monitoring of balance changes, tracking of ownership transfers, and validation of critical state transitions.

Integration monitoring requires attention when contracts interact with external systems. Proper tracking of external calls, monitoring of response patterns, and validation of interaction results help maintain system reliability. This includes monitoring oracle interactions, tracking cross contract calls, and validating external data sources.

Performance monitoring helps maintain efficient contract operations. Systems should track execution times, monitor resource usage, and identify potential bottlenecks. This includes proper analysis of function execution patterns, monitoring of computational resource usage, and identification of performance optimization opportunities.

Security monitoring forms a critical aspect of post deployment operations. Systems should implement proper security checks, maintain intrusion detection capabilities, and provide immediate alerts for potential security issues. This includes monitoring of unauthorized access attempts, tracking of suspicious patterns, and validation of security constraints.

Error monitoring helps identify and address operational issues quickly. Systems should track error occurrences, maintain proper error logs, and provide detailed information about failure conditions. This includes proper tracking of revert conditions, monitoring of exception patterns, and analysis of error frequencies.

User impact monitoring helps maintain service quality. Systems should track user success rates, monitor failed transactions, and identify patterns that might indicate usability issues. This includes proper analysis of transaction success rates, monitoring of user interaction patterns, and identification of potential improvement areas.

Resource utilization monitoring ensures efficient contract operations. Systems should track storage usage, monitor computational resources, and identify potential optimization opportunities. This includes proper analysis of storage patterns, monitoring of computation costs, and identification of resource optimization possibilities.

Dependency monitoring becomes important for contracts that rely on external systems. Teams should track the status of dependent contracts, monitor integration points, and validate external service availability. This includes proper monitoring of oracle services, tracking of external contract states, and validation of critical dependencies.

Regulatory compliance monitoring ensures continued adherence to relevant requirements. Systems should track compliance related metrics, maintain proper audit trails, and provide necessary reporting capabilities. This includes monitoring of regulatory thresholds, tracking of compliance related events, and maintenance of required documentation.

Market impact monitoring becomes crucial for contracts handling financial operations. Systems should track price impacts, monitor liquidity patterns, and identify potential market manipulation attempts. This includes proper analysis of trading patterns, monitoring of price movements, and identification of suspicious activities.

Technical debt monitoring helps maintain contract health over time. Systems should track code complexity metrics, monitor maintenance needs, and identify areas requiring updates. This includes proper analysis of contract structure, monitoring of update requirements, and identification of improvement opportunities.

Documentation monitoring ensures continued accuracy of system documentation. Teams should track documentation updates, maintain proper version control, and ensure alignment with current implementations. This includes monitoring of documentation accuracy, tracking of implementation changes, and maintenance of proper documentation standards.

The implementation of effective post deployment monitoring requires careful attention to multiple aspects of contract operations. Regular review and updates of monitoring systems ensure continued effectiveness as contract usage evolves. Proper consideration of these aspects helps maintain secure and efficient smart contract operations in production environments.

61. Contract Maintenance Patterns

Contract maintenance patterns represent a crucial aspect of managing smart contracts throughout their lifecycle. These patterns help ensure contracts remain secure, efficient, and adaptable to changing requirements while maintaining operational stability.

The foundation of effective contract maintenance begins with implementing proper versioning mechanisms. Contracts should maintain clear version identifiers, implement structured upgrade paths, and provide proper migration capabilities. This enables teams to track contract evolution, manage updates effectively, and maintain proper system documentation throughout the contract lifecycle.

State management patterns form a critical component of contract maintenance. Contracts should implement proper state isolation, maintain clear state transitions, and provide mechanisms for state validation. This includes implementing proper storage patterns, managing state dependencies, and ensuring data integrity across contract updates. Effective state management patterns help prevent data corruption, maintain system consistency, and facilitate smooth contract upgrades.

Modular design patterns significantly enhance maintainability. Contracts should be structured with clear separation of concerns, implement proper interface definitions, and maintain loose coupling between components. This architectural approach allows teams to update specific functionality without affecting the entire system, reduce testing complexity, and maintain better code organization. Modular patterns also facilitate easier bug fixes and feature additions while minimizing the risk of introducing new vulnerabilities.

Diagnostic capabilities represent an essential maintenance pattern. Contracts should implement proper debugging functions, maintain comprehensive event logging, and provide mechanisms for system analysis. These capabilities help teams identify issues quickly, understand system behavior, and implement effective solutions. Proper diagnostic patterns include read only functions for state inspection, events for tracking critical operations, and mechanisms for analyzing system performance.

Update mechanisms require careful consideration in maintenance patterns. Contracts should implement proper upgrade paths, maintain backward compatibility where possible, and provide clear migration procedures. This includes implementing proxy patterns when needed, managing storage layouts carefully, and ensuring proper handling of existing data during upgrades. Effective update patterns help maintain system stability while allowing necessary improvements and modifications.

Error handling patterns play a crucial role in maintenance. Contracts should implement proper error recovery mechanisms, maintain clear error states, and provide appropriate fallback behaviors. This includes implementing proper revert conditions, managing error propagation, and ensuring system stability during error conditions. Robust error handling patterns help maintain system reliability and facilitate easier problem resolution.

Configuration management patterns help adapt contracts to changing requirements. Contracts should implement proper parameter management, maintain configuration flexibility, and provide mechanisms for adjusting system behavior. This includes implementing governor patterns for parameter updates, managing system constants effectively, and providing mechanisms for behavioral adaptation. Effective configuration patterns help maintain system flexibility while ensuring proper security controls.

Testing support patterns facilitate ongoing maintenance activities. Contracts should implement proper test hooks, maintain testing interfaces, and provide mechanisms for validation. This includes implementing proper assertion mechanisms, maintaining test states, and providing capabilities for system verification. Strong testing patterns help ensure continued system reliability through various maintenance activities.

Documentation maintenance patterns ensure continued system understanding. Contracts should maintain proper code comments, implement clear function documentation, and provide comprehensive system descriptions. This includes maintaining proper NatSpec documentation, providing clear architectural descriptions, and ensuring documentation remains synchronized with implementations. Effective documentation patterns help maintain system knowledge and facilitate future maintenance activities.

Access control maintenance patterns ensure continued security. Contracts should implement proper role management, maintain permission structures, and provide mechanisms for access updates. This includes implementing proper authorization patterns, managing administrative capabilities, and ensuring secure access modifications. Robust access control patterns help maintain system security throughout the contract lifecycle.

Monitoring support patterns facilitate ongoing system observation. Contracts should implement proper metric collection, maintain system statistics, and provide mechanisms for operational analysis. This includes implementing proper event structures, maintaining operational counters, and providing mechanisms for system analysis. Effective monitoring patterns help maintain system visibility and facilitate proactive maintenance.

Resource management patterns ensure continued efficiency. Contracts should implement proper resource allocation, maintain usage tracking, and provide optimization capabilities. This includes implementing proper storage management, maintaining gas efficiency, and providing mechanisms for resource optimization. Strong resource management patterns help maintain system performance through various maintenance activities.

Integration maintenance patterns manage external dependencies. Contracts should implement proper interface management, maintain integration flexibility, and provide mechanisms for adapting to external changes. This includes implementing proper abstract contracts, managing dependency versions, and providing mechanisms for integration updates. Effective integration patterns help maintain system stability when external components change.

Recovery patterns provide mechanisms for handling serious issues. Contracts should implement proper emergency procedures, maintain system safeguards, and provide mechanisms for critical interventions. This includes implementing circuit breakers, maintaining recovery procedures, and providing mechanisms for system restoration. Robust recovery patterns help maintain system resilience through various operational challenges.

Governance patterns facilitate systematic maintenance processes. Contracts should implement proper decision making mechanisms, maintain upgrade procedures, and provide mechanisms for coordinated changes. This includes implementing proper voting systems, maintaining proposal mechanisms, and providing structured update processes. Effective governance patterns help maintain orderly system evolution while ensuring proper stakeholder involvement.

The implementation of these maintenance patterns requires careful consideration of system requirements, security implications, and operational needs. Regular review and refinement of maintenance patterns ensure their continued effectiveness as system requirements evolve. Proper attention to these patterns helps maintain secure, efficient, and adaptable smart contract systems throughout their operational lifecycle.

62. Future-Proofing Strategies

Future proofing strategies in smart contract development require careful consideration of both technical and operational aspects to ensure contracts remain viable, secure, and efficient over extended periods. This chapter explores comprehensive approaches to building contracts that can withstand the test of time and adapt to evolving blockchain ecosystems.

Extensibility serves as a cornerstone of future proofing smart contracts. Contracts must be designed with extension points that allow for the addition of new functionality without disrupting existing operations. This involves implementing proper interface definitions, maintaining clear upgrade paths, and establishing flexible architectural patterns that can accommodate future requirements. Developers should consider implementing abstract contracts and utilizing inheritance patterns that facilitate feature additions while maintaining backward compatibility.

Data structure flexibility plays a crucial role in future proofing. Contracts should implement storage patterns that can accommodate potential data model changes, maintain proper versioning of data structures, and provide mechanisms for data migration. This includes implementing mappings that can handle additional fields, utilizing proper storage slots for upgradeable contracts, and maintaining clear data access patterns that can evolve over time. Careful consideration of storage patterns helps ensure contracts can adapt to changing data requirements without requiring complete system rebuilds.

Protocol adaptation capabilities ensure contracts can evolve with the underlying blockchain ecosystem. This involves implementing proper abstraction layers for protocol specific functionality, maintaining flexibility in consensus mechanisms, and providing capabilities to adapt to network upgrades. Developers should consider implementing protocol agnostic interfaces, maintaining proper fallback mechanisms, and ensuring contracts can handle potential changes in network parameters or transaction formats.

Scalability considerations form an essential aspect of future proofing. Contracts should implement proper batch processing capabilities, maintain efficient data structures, and provide mechanisms for handling increased transaction volumes. This includes implementing proper pagination patterns, maintaining optimized storage layouts, and ensuring contracts can handle growing user bases and transaction frequencies. Proper attention to scalability helps ensure contracts remain viable as usage patterns evolve.

Interoperability features ensure contracts can interact with evolving ecosystem standards. This involves implementing proper interface standards, maintaining flexibility in external interactions, and providing mechanisms for adapting to new protocols. Developers should consider implementing abstract interfaces for external interactions, maintaining proper versioning of integration points, and ensuring contracts can adapt to changes in external systems or standards.

Security adaptability represents a critical future proofing consideration. Contracts should implement flexible security patterns, maintain updatable security mechanisms, and provide capabilities for implementing new security features. This includes implementing proper access control abstractions, maintaining upgradeable security modules, and ensuring contracts can incorporate new security best practices as they emerge. Regular security reviews and updates help maintain long term contract viability.

Performance optimization flexibility ensures contracts can adapt to changing efficiency requirements. This involves implementing proper optimization hooks, maintaining performance monitoring capabilities, and providing mechanisms for implementing efficiency improvements. Developers should consider implementing optimizable components, maintaining proper benchmarking capabilities, and ensuring contracts can incorporate new optimization techniques as they become available.

Governance adaptability enables contracts to evolve with changing organizational requirements. This involves implementing flexible decision making mechanisms, maintaining adaptable upgrade procedures, and providing capabilities for evolving governance models. Proper attention to governance flexibility helps ensure contracts can accommodate changing stakeholder needs and regulatory requirements over time.

Economic model flexibility allows contracts to adapt to changing market conditions. This involves implementing adjustable economic parameters, maintaining proper incentive structures, and providing mechanisms for modifying economic models. Developers should consider implementing parametrized economic functions, maintaining proper economic controls, and ensuring contracts can adapt to evolving market dynamics.

Testing adaptability ensures contracts can maintain quality assurance as requirements evolve. This involves implementing flexible testing frameworks, maintaining proper test coverage, and providing capabilities for implementing new testing approaches. This includes implementing proper test interfaces, maintaining comprehensive test suites, and ensuring contracts can incorporate new testing methodologies as they emerge.

Documentation adaptability facilitates ongoing system understanding. This involves implementing proper documentation generation, maintaining clear architectural descriptions, and providing mechanisms for evolving documentation. Developers should consider implementing self documenting patterns, maintaining proper documentation tooling, and ensuring documentation can evolve with the system.

Integration flexibility ensures contracts can adapt to changing external systems. This involves implementing proper integration abstractions, maintaining flexible integration points, and providing capabilities for adapting to new integration requirements. This includes implementing proper interface abstractions, maintaining integration versioning, and ensuring contracts can accommodate changes in external dependencies.

Resource management flexibility allows contracts to adapt to changing resource requirements. This involves implementing adjustable resource allocation, maintaining proper usage tracking, and providing mechanisms for resource optimization. Developers should consider implementing flexible resource limits, maintaining proper resource monitoring, and ensuring contracts can adapt to changing resource availability.

Monitoring adaptability ensures continued operational visibility. This involves implementing flexible monitoring interfaces, maintaining proper metric collection, and providing capabilities for implementing new monitoring approaches. This includes implementing proper event structures, maintaining operational analytics, and ensuring contracts can incorporate new monitoring requirements.

These future proofing strategies require careful balance between flexibility and complexity. While implementing these strategies, developers must maintain proper security controls, ensure system stability, and avoid unnecessary complexity that could introduce vulnerabilities. Regular review and refinement of future proofing strategies helps ensure their continued effectiveness as system requirements evolve.

Success in future proofing smart contracts ultimately depends on maintaining a proper balance between current functionality and future adaptability. This involves careful consideration of system requirements, proper implementation of flexible patterns, and regular review of system capabilities against evolving needs. Through proper attention to these strategies, developers can create contracts that remain viable and valuable over extended periods while maintaining security and efficiency.

63. Regulatory Compliance

Regulatory compliance in smart contract development has become increasingly important as blockchain technology matures and attracts greater scrutiny from regulatory bodies worldwide. This chapter explores the essential considerations and implementation strategies for ensuring smart contracts meet regulatory requirements while maintaining their decentralized and innovative nature.

Understanding the regulatory landscape forms the foundation of compliance efforts. Smart contract developers must navigate various regulatory frameworks, including securities laws, anti-money laundering (AML) regulations, know your customer (KYC) requirements, and data protection standards. Different jurisdictions may impose varying requirements, necessitating flexible implementation approaches that can accommodate multiple regulatory regimes.

Identity verification represents a crucial compliance component for many smart contract applications. Implementations must consider appropriate methods for user verification, credential management, and privacy protection. This often involves integrating with external identity verification services, implementing proper data handling procedures, and maintaining audit trails of verification processes. Developers must balance regulatory requirements with user privacy concerns, implementing solutions that satisfy compliance needs while protecting sensitive information.

Transaction monitoring capabilities play a vital role in regulatory compliance. Smart contracts must implement proper transaction tracking, maintain comprehensive audit trails, and provide mechanisms for detecting suspicious activities. This includes implementing transaction logging systems, maintaining proper monitoring interfaces, and ensuring contracts can identify and report potential compliance violations. Proper attention to transaction monitoring helps ensure ongoing regulatory adherence while facilitating necessary reporting requirements.

Data protection compliance has become increasingly important with the introduction of regulations like GDPR and CCPA. Smart contracts must implement proper data handling procedures, maintain user privacy controls, and provide mechanisms for data subject rights. This involves implementing proper data encryption, maintaining access controls, and ensuring contracts can accommodate user requests for data modification or deletion. Careful consideration of data protection requirements helps ensure compliance while maintaining system functionality.

Financial compliance requirements often necessitate specific implementation patterns. Smart contracts must implement proper financial controls, maintain transaction limits, and provide mechanisms for financial reporting. This includes implementing proper asset handling procedures, maintaining financial audit trails, and ensuring contracts can generate required financial reports. Developers must consider various financial regulations, including securities laws, banking regulations, and tax requirements.

Reporting capabilities form an essential component of regulatory compliance. Smart contracts must implement proper event logging, maintain comprehensive activity records, and provide mechanisms for generating regulatory reports. This involves implementing proper event structures, maintaining historical data access, and ensuring contracts can produce required compliance documentation. Regular review of reporting requirements helps ensure continued regulatory adherence.

Geographic restrictions often require specific implementation considerations. Smart contracts must implement proper jurisdiction controls, maintain geographic access limitations, and provide mechanisms for enforcing regional requirements. This includes implementing proper location verification, maintaining jurisdiction specific parameters, and ensuring contracts can adapt to varying regional regulations. Careful attention to geographic compliance helps prevent unauthorized access while maintaining proper service delivery.

Governance compliance requires specific implementation patterns. Smart contracts must implement proper decision making procedures, maintain stakeholder controls, and provide mechanisms for regulatory oversight. This involves implementing proper voting mechanisms, maintaining governance records, and ensuring contracts can accommodate regulatory intervention when required. Proper attention to governance compliance helps ensure continued regulatory acceptance while maintaining operational effectiveness.

Consumer protection measures form an important compliance consideration. Smart contracts must implement proper user safeguards, maintain consumer rights mechanisms, and provide appropriate dispute resolution capabilities. This includes implementing proper user controls, maintaining consumer protection features, and ensuring contracts can handle user complaints and disputes effectively. Regular review of consumer protection requirements helps ensure continued compliance while maintaining user trust.

Securities compliance often requires specific implementation approaches. Smart contracts must implement proper securities handling procedures, maintain appropriate investor controls, and provide mechanisms for securities regulation compliance. This includes implementing proper token standards, maintaining investor verification, and ensuring contracts can accommodate securities trading requirements. Careful consideration of securities regulations helps ensure proper market operation while maintaining regulatory compliance.

Anti money laundering compliance requires specific implementation patterns. Smart contracts must implement proper transaction monitoring, maintain appropriate verification procedures, and provide mechanisms for detecting potential money laundering activities. This involves implementing proper transaction controls, maintaining verification records, and ensuring contracts can identify suspicious patterns. Regular review of AML requirements helps ensure continued compliance while maintaining system security.

Tax compliance considerations require specific implementation approaches. Smart contracts must implement proper transaction recording, maintain appropriate financial tracking, and provide mechanisms for tax reporting. This includes implementing proper accounting functions, maintaining transaction histories, and ensuring contracts can generate required tax documentation. Careful attention to tax requirements helps ensure proper financial reporting while maintaining operational efficiency.

Compliance documentation plays a crucial role in regulatory adherence. Smart contracts must implement proper documentation generation, maintain comprehensive compliance records, and provide mechanisms for regulatory review. This involves implementing proper documentation systems, maintaining compliance histories, and ensuring contracts can demonstrate regulatory adherence when required. Regular review of documentation requirements helps ensure continued compliance while maintaining system transparency.

Regulatory compliance in smart contract development requires ongoing attention and adaptation. As regulatory requirements evolve, contracts must maintain flexibility while ensuring continued compliance. This involves regular review of regulatory changes, proper implementation of compliance updates, and maintenance of comprehensive compliance programs. Through proper attention to regulatory requirements, developers can create contracts that maintain compliance while delivering intended functionality.

Success in regulatory compliance ultimately depends on maintaining proper balance between innovation and regulatory adherence. This involves careful consideration of regulatory requirements, proper implementation of compliance measures, and regular review of compliance effectiveness. Through proper attention to these considerations, developers can create contracts that satisfy regulatory requirements while maintaining their innovative potential and operational efficiency.

64. Security Tools and Resources

The landscape of smart contract security tools and resources continues to evolve rapidly, providing developers with an increasingly sophisticated arsenal for creating secure decentralized applications. This chapter explores the essential tools, platforms, and resources available for enhancing smart contract security throughout the development lifecycle.

Static analysis tools form the foundation of automated security testing. Tools like Slither, Mythril, and SmartCheck provide automated vulnerability detection capabilities, analyzing smart contract code for common security issues. These tools employ various analysis techniques, from pattern matching to symbolic execution, helping developers identify potential vulnerabilities before deployment. Understanding the strengths and limitations of each tool enables developers to implement comprehensive security testing strategies.

Development environments and frameworks play a crucial role in secure contract creation. Frameworks like Hardhat, Truffle, and Brownie provide robust development environments with built-in security features, testing capabilities, and deployment tools. These frameworks often include security plugins and extensions that enhance their security testing capabilities, making them invaluable for maintaining security throughout the development process.

Verification platforms provide essential tools for formal verification and mathematical proof of contract correctness. Platforms like Certora, Act, and K Framework enable developers to specify and verify contract properties mathematically. These tools help ensure that smart contracts behave exactly as intended under all possible conditions, providing a higher level of security assurance than traditional testing methods alone.

Security monitoring services offer ongoing contract surveillance and threat detection. Platforms like Forta, OpenZeppelin Defender, and Tenderly provide real-time monitoring capabilities, alerting developers to potential security incidents or unusual contract behavior. These services help maintain security post-deployment, enabling quick response to potential threats or vulnerabilities.

Documentation and learning resources provide essential knowledge for security-conscious development. Platforms like OpenZeppelin Docs, Ethereum Security Documentation, and various security-focused blogs offer comprehensive guidance on secure development practices. These resources help developers stay informed about emerging security threats and best practices while providing practical implementation guidance.

Audit platforms and services offer professional security review capabilities. Companies like Trail of Bits, ConsenSys Diligence, and Quantstamp provide comprehensive smart contract auditing services. Understanding these services' capabilities and requirements helps developers prepare for successful audits while maintaining high security standards throughout development.

Testing frameworks provide essential tools for security testing implementation. Frameworks like Waffle, Foundry, and dapp.tools offer robust testing capabilities specifically designed for smart contract development. These tools enable comprehensive security testing, including unit tests, integration tests, and security-specific test scenarios.

Gas optimization tools help developers maintain efficiency while implementing security measures. Tools like eth-gas-reporter and hardhat-gas-reporter provide detailed gas usage analysis, helping developers optimize contract efficiency without compromising security. Understanding these tools helps developers balance security requirements with operational efficiency.

Contract verification services provide important tools for code transparency and verification. Platforms like Etherscan and Sourcify enable developers to verify and publish contract source code, enhancing transparency and enabling community security review. These services play a crucial role in maintaining trust and enabling thorough security analysis.

Vulnerability databases and security advisories provide essential information about known security issues. Resources like SWC Registry and Ethereum Smart Contract Security Registry maintain comprehensive information about smart contract vulnerabilities and attack vectors. These resources help developers understand and protect against known security threats.

Development tools often include security-specific features and capabilities. Tools like Remix IDE include built-in security analyzers and verification tools, while VSCode extensions provide security-focused development capabilities. Understanding these tools' security features helps developers maintain security throughout the development process.

Blockchain explorers and analysis tools provide important contract monitoring capabilities. Platforms like Etherscan, Bloxy, and Dune Analytics offer detailed contract analysis and monitoring features. These tools help developers track contract behavior and identify potential security issues in deployed contracts.

Community resources play a vital role in security knowledge sharing. Forums, Discord channels, and security-focused communities provide valuable platforms for discussing security issues and sharing knowledge. These resources help developers stay informed about emerging security threats and best practices while enabling collaborative problem solving.

Security standards and guidelines provide essential frameworks for secure development. Resources like the Smart Contract Security Verification Standard (SCSVS) and various security checklists offer comprehensive guidance for maintaining security throughout development. These resources help ensure consistent security practices while providing practical implementation guidance.

Deployment and testing networks provide essential environments for security testing. Networks like Goerli and Sepolia enable thorough testing before mainnet deployment, while local networks enable detailed security testing during development. Understanding these resources helps developers maintain comprehensive security testing throughout the development lifecycle.

The landscape of smart contract security tools and resources continues to evolve, with new tools and capabilities emerging regularly. Staying informed about available resources and maintaining familiarity with essential tools helps developers create more secure smart contracts while enabling efficient security implementation. Through proper utilization of these resources, developers can enhance their security practices while maintaining development efficiency.

65. Case Studies and Lessons Learned

In this chapter, we explore several illuminating case studies from the smart contract security landscape and extract valuable lessons that can guide future development practices. These real-world examples demonstrate both successful security implementations and costly failures, providing concrete insights into effective security strategies.

The DAO hack of 2016 remains one of the most significant case studies in smart contract security. The incident, which resulted in the loss of approximately 3.6 million ETH, highlighted the critical importance of thorough security testing and the dangers of reentrancy vulnerabilities. The attack exploited a recursive call vulnerability in the withdrawal function, allowing attackers to repeatedly withdraw funds before the contract could update its balance. This case demonstrates the importance of implementing checks-effects-interactions pattern and thorough testing of state-changing functions.

Parity's multi-signature wallet incident in 2017 provides another crucial lesson in contract security. A vulnerability in the wallet's library contract allowed an attacker to gain ownership and subsequently destroy it, rendering multiple wallets unusable and freezing millions of dollars worth of assets. This case emphasizes the importance of careful library contract implementation and proper access control mechanisms. It also highlights the risks associated with shared library contracts and the need for thorough testing of initialization functions.

The Poly Network hack of 2021, resulting in the temporary loss of over $600 million in assets, demonstrates the importance of proper access control and cross-chain interaction security. The attack exploited vulnerabilities in the cross-chain messaging system, allowing the attacker to forge messages and manipulate contract ownership. This case highlights the complexity of securing cross-chain interactions and the need for robust verification mechanisms in cross-chain protocols.

The Compound protocol's distribution bug in 2021 offers lessons in upgrade management and testing. An error in an upgrade resulted in incorrect token distributions worth millions of dollars. This incident demonstrates the importance of comprehensive testing for contract upgrades, including edge cases and different scenarios. It also highlights the value of gradual rollouts and emergency stop mechanisms in protocol upgrades.

The Cream Finance flash loan attacks in 2021 provide insights into DeFi security considerations. Multiple attacks exploiting price oracle vulnerabilities and flash loan mechanics resulted in substantial losses. These incidents highlight the importance of robust price oracle implementation and careful consideration of flash loan attack vectors in DeFi protocols.

The Wormhole bridge hack in 2022, resulting in the loss of $320 million, demonstrates the criticality of proper signature verification and cross-chain communication security. The attack exploited vulnerabilities in the bridge's verification system, allowing the creation of unbacked tokens. This case emphasizes the importance of thorough validation mechanisms in bridge protocols and the risks associated with cross-chain asset transfers.

Successful security implementations also provide valuable lessons. The MakerDAO system's resilience during the March 2020 crypto market crash demonstrates the importance of robust system design and careful risk management. The protocol's ability to handle extreme market conditions while maintaining stability highlights the value of comprehensive stress testing and emergency response mechanisms.

The Uniswap protocol's security track record offers insights into successful security implementation. Despite handling billions in transaction volume, the core protocol has maintained a strong security record through careful design, thorough testing, and gradual deployment strategies. This success demonstrates the value of security-first development approaches and comprehensive testing strategies.

OpenZeppelin's implementation of upgradeable contracts provides lessons in successful upgrade pattern implementation. Their transparent proxy pattern has become an industry standard, demonstrating the importance of well-designed upgrade mechanisms and thorough documentation. This case highlights the value of standardized security patterns and community-reviewed implementations.

The Chainlink oracle network's security implementation offers insights into successful oracle security. Their decentralized oracle network has maintained reliability through multiple market stress events, demonstrating the importance of robust oracle design and careful security implementation in critical infrastructure components.

These case studies reveal several common themes in successful security implementation. Thorough testing, including edge cases and stress scenarios, proves consistently crucial. Careful access control implementation, including multi-signature mechanisms and time locks, helps prevent unauthorized actions. Gradual deployment strategies and emergency stop mechanisms provide important safety nets during upgrades and emergencies.

The lessons learned also highlight the importance of security-first development approaches. Prioritizing security during initial design and development often proves more effective than attempting to add security measures later. Regular security audits, both internal and external, help identify potential vulnerabilities before they can be exploited.

Documentation and transparency emerge as crucial elements in successful security implementation. Clear documentation of security measures, potential risks, and incident response procedures helps maintain security throughout a project's lifecycle. Transparency about security practices and incident handling helps build trust and enables community participation in security maintenance.

Community engagement and responsible disclosure programs have proven valuable in maintaining security. Many successful projects maintain bug bounty programs and engage actively with security researchers, helping identify and address potential vulnerabilities before they can be exploited.

The evolution of security practices across these cases demonstrates the importance of continuous learning and adaptation. Successful projects consistently update their security practices based on new threats and lessons learned, maintaining robust security through changing conditions.

These case studies and lessons continue to inform security best practices in smart contract development. By understanding and applying these lessons, developers can create more secure smart contracts while avoiding known pitfalls and vulnerabilities. The ongoing accumulation of security knowledge through real-world experiences helps advance the field's understanding of effective security practices.

Don't miss out!

Visit the website below and you can sign up to receive emails whenever Pete Cox publishes a new book. There's no charge and no obligation.

https://books2read.com/r/B-A-PWDVC-TPKIF

BOOKS 2 READ

Connecting independent readers to independent writers.

About the Publisher

Northwood Lore Books is an independent imprint dedicated to producing accessible, thought-provoking content through the use of advanced content generation systems. All books published under this imprint are created for educational or entertainment purposes only. Authors listed under this imprint use pen names and are not subject-matter experts. Accordingly, no material should be interpreted as financial, legal, medical, or professional advice. The information provided is general in nature, subject to change, and may not reflect the most current data or guidance. Readers are encouraged to consult official sources or qualified professionals before making decisions based on the content herein.

www.ingramcontent.com/pod-product-compliance
Lightning Source LLC
LaVergne TN
LVHW090315210926
848480LV00001B/261